Culver McSparren Connection

Ancestors of Tad D. Culver

Betmatrho Genealogy Publications

Culver - McSparren Connection
Ancestors of Tad D. Culver

First Printing August 27, 2017

Betmatrho Publications
29252 Brush Creek Road
California, Missouri 65018
http://the-red-thread.net/

To obtain additional copies of this book contact me at:
betmatrho3@gmail.com

Culver Origins and Coat of Arms (Displayed on Front Cover of this booklet)

SURNAME ORIGINS: English
Spelling variations of this family name include: Culver, Culvere and others. First found in Herefordshire where they were seated from very ancient times, some say before the Norman Conquest in 1066. Some of the first settlers of this family name or some of its variants were: Edward Culver of Dedham, Massachusetts, was a wheelwright who settled there before 1640. He and his family moved to New London, CT about 1653; W. B. Culver settled in San Francisco Cal. in 1850.

CREST: A tower with a dove with wings expanded.
COAT OF ARMS: A black shield with an ermine fesse between three silver doves.

Table of Contents

Table of Contents

TAD CULVER
Chorus 1; Dance 2,3; Pro-
jectionist 2,3,4; Student
Council 4. Future Sales-
man . . . Happy Go Lucky
. . . Belongs to "Short
Senior Gal" . . . Loses
Books . . . Likes Mrs. Com-
stock.

ANCESTORS OF TAD DAVID CULVER

Generation No. 1

1. *Tad David Culver*, born April 30, 1941 in Warren Twp, Trumbull County, Ohio. He is the son of **2. Leo Virgil Culver** and **3. Helen Pearl McSparren**. Tad went to Wattsburg Schools and lived in Wattsburg until his wife died in 2001. He now lives in North East, PA area. Tad married Marilyn Mae Matteson on April 1, 1960 at Wattsburg Methodist Church in Wattsburg, Erie County, Pennsylvania.

(1) Marilyn Mae Matteson, born August 27, 1943 at Corry Hospital, Corry, Erie County, Pennsylvania. Marilyn went to Wattsburg Schools and lived in the area all her life. She died on July 25, 2001 in Erie, Erie County, PA and is buried at Wattsburg Cemetery. She was the daughter of Rodney 'Pete' Carl Matteson and Ethel Mae Hoag.

Tad & Marilyn Culver have 5 children:

1. **Troy David Culver** married Christine Louise DiSanti and they have two children, Philip and Amber.
2. **Susanne Renee Culver** 1st married Timothy Nicewonger and they have three children, Elizabeth, Andrew & Emily. Tim & Susie divorced and she is now married to William T. Hussey.
3. **Brett Vincent Culver (Sgt 1st Class)** married Yvonne Marie Green and they have one son, Jack.
4. **Craig Steven Culver** married Tina Firestone and they have three children, Erica, Adam & Darcy.
5. **Matthew Tad Culver** married Margaret 'Peggy' Ann Collins and they have two children, Matthew II & Mary Ann 'Molly'.

Additional notes:
Tad's middle name "DAVID" was his maternal grandfather, David William McSparren's, first name.

"Marilyn Matteson Culver - Service will be held Saturday

Marilyn M. Culver, 57, 14368 Church St., Wattsburg, died Wednesday, July 25, 2001, at IHS Erie at Bayside after a lengthy illness. She was born in Corry, daughter of Ethel Mae Hoag Matteson of Corry and the late Rodney "Pete" Matteson. She enjoyed gardening, cooking, sewing and crafts. She was preceded in death by a brother, Fred Matteson. Survivors include her husband, Tad Culver; four sons, Troy Culver and his wife, Tina, of Lake City, U.S. Army Sgt. 1st Class Brett Culver and his wife, Yvonne, of Fairview Township, Craig Culver and his wife, Tina, of North East and Matthew Culver and his wife, Peggy, of Erie; a daughter, Suzanne Hussey and her husband, Bill, of Wattsburg; three brothers, John Matteson of North East, Bill Matteson of Erie and Bob Matteson of Corry; four sisters, Betty Rhodes of California, MO., Kathy Stahlman and Judy Wilcox, both of Corry, and Alice Meade of North East; 10 grandchilcren; and several nieces and nephews. Friends may call today from 7 to 9 p.m. and Friday from 2 to 5 and 7 to 9 p.m. at the Pine Avenue Branch of the A. Brugger & Sons Funeral Home, 845 E. 38th St. A service will be held there Saturday at 10 a.m., officated by the Rev. Raymond Speakman. Burial will be at Wattsburg Cemetery."

Notes for Marilyn Mae Matteson:
Find A Grave Memorial# 5638711

Generation No. 2

(Parents)

2.   *Leo Virgil Culver*, (Reverend), born December 13, 1921 in Edinboro, Erie County, Pennsylvania. Leo lived for a short time in Trumbull Co, Ohio before settling down in Oklahoma where he made his home. Leo died on March 04, 2010 in Grove, Delaware Co, Oklahoma and is buried at the Olympus Cemetery. He was the son of 4. Carl Dewey Culver and 5. Olive Madeline DeRemer. He married/partnered with 3. Helen Pearl McSparren sometime prior to 1941. Leo married/partnered a 2nd time to Ione Shampoe about 1944.

3.   *Helen Pearl McSparren*, born October 17, 1919 in Emlenton, (which is partly in Clariton County and partly in Venango County), she lists her birth as being in Clariton Co, Pennsylvania. Growing up, she lived in Sugarcreek, Venango Co, Pennsylvania and spent a short time in Ohio where her son Tad, was born. Helen married c.1973 a man by the name of Walker, but never found his first name. She spent several years in the Warren State Hospital and died there on January 14, 1999 in Warren, Warren Co, Pennsylvania. She is buried at Warren State Hospital Cemetery. She was the daughter of 6. David William Sutton McSparren and 7. Annetta 'Nettie' Bell Umstead.

Burial infor for Leo Virgil Culver:
Find A Grave Memorial# 157445846
Burial info for Helen Pearl McSparren:
Find A Grave Memorial# 86428998

1930 census, Leo V. Culver, age 8, is living at Rockland, Venango County, Pennsylvania with Uncle Raymond S. Stroup (age 54) & Ray's wife, Pearl D. Stroup, and their son, Cleo S. Stroup.
1940 census, did not find Leo on the 1940 census, nor did I find Helen P. McSparren.

Helen's Social Security Application and changes made:
Name: Helen Pearl Walker; [Helen Walker]; [Helen Pearl McSparren]
SSN: 172522362
Gender: Female Race: White
Birth Date: 17 Oct 1919   Birth Place: Emelenton Clarion, Pennsylvania
Death Date: 14 Jan 1999
Father: David McSparren Mother: Nettie McSparren
Type of Claim: Original SSN.
Relationship of Signature: Not signed, SSA prepared.
Notes: 27 Dec 1973: Name listed as HELEN PEARL WALKER
Notes: 02 Feb 1999: Name listed as HELEN WALKER

1930 Census - Helen P. McSparren age 9, living in Sugar Creek Twp, Venango Co, PA with parents & siblings.

Child of Leo Culver and Helen McSparren is:

1   i. Tad David Culver, born April 30, 1941 in Warren Twp, Trumbull Co, Ohio; he married Marilyn Mae Matteson April 01, 1961 in Wattsburg, PA.

Children of Leo Culver and Ione Shampoe:

 i. Cheryl Darlene Culver b. June 30, 1945 in Corry, Erie Co, Pennsylvania
 ii. Shelby Maureen Culver b. July 29, 1946 in Corry, Erie Co, Pennsylvania
 iii. Keith Larue Culver b. January 3, 1948 in Union City, Erie Co, Pennsylvania

School District No. 18 School District Name ____ County Ottawa
Name of Parent (or Guardian): Rev. Leo Culver Post Office Commerce
Home Owner ____ Tenant ✓ Occupation: Reverend
Name of Tribe (if Indian): ____ (See instructions for Col. 3). Indian Parents Live Within City Limits Yes ( ) No ( )

1 NAME OF CHILD	2 GRADE IN SCHOOL	3 SEX M	3 SEX F	4 DATE OF BIRTH Mo.	Day	Yr.	5 AGE Sept. 1	6 PLACE OF BIRTH City & State	*7 17a	**8 NATURE OF DISABILITY	9 PREVENTS SCHOOL ATTENDANCE
Culver, Keith LaRue	8	✓		1	3	1948	14	Union City, Pa.			
Culver, Shelby Maureen	10		✓	7	29	1946	16	Corry, Pa.			
Culver, Cheryl Darlene	11		✓	6	30	1945	17	Corry, Pa.			

Children who are 17 but will be 18 on or before September 1.
Disabilities: Blind, Near Blind, Crippled, Deaf, Epileptic, Hard of Hearing, Mentally Deficient, Speech Deficiency, Heart Trouble, or Other Disability.
I hereby declare under oath that the above is a true and correct statement of the facts given; that I am a legal resident of the above school district and the names and ages of all persons are correct as written above.
Subscribed and sworn to before me the 11 day of April 19 62 Father or Mother Mrs Leo V. Culver
Mrs. Harold H. Hart Guardian or Custodian ____
Enumerator Form R-C 1

Generation No. 3

(Grandparents)
Found: 4 of 4

4. *Carl Dewey Culver*, born June 22, 1898 in Venango County, Pennsylvania, also lived in Meadville, West Mead Twp, Crawford Co, PA and in Warren, Ohio. Carl died September 12, 1993 in Manatee Co, Florida and is buried at the Manasota Memorial Park Cemetery at Bradenton, Florida. He was the son of 8. Carson Earl Culver and 9. Mabel Mae Holt. He married 5. Olive Madeline DeRemer on June 15, 1918 in Meadville, Crawford Co, Pennsylvania. Carl married a 2nd time to Clara Hazel Doerfer.

5. *Olive Madeline DeRemer*, born January 16, 1899 in Blooming Valley Twp, Crawford Co, Pennsylvania. Olive died at Jamestown General Hospital in Chautauqua Co, New York on February 05, 1975. Her residence was Meadville, Crawford Co, PA prior to being admitted to the hospital. She is buried at Blooming Valley Cemetery. She was the daughter of 10. George William DeRemer and 11. Minnie Mae Clark.

Burial notes for Carl Dewey Culver:
Find A Grave Memorial# 125331835
Burial notes for Olive Madeline DeRemer:
Find A Grave Memorial# 151955591
Burial notes for Hazel C. Culver:
Find A Grave Memorial# 125331840

1900 Census, Carrol D. (*Carl D.*) age 2 living with parents and twin brothers at Oakland Twp, Venango Co, PA.
1910 Census, Carl D. Culver, age 11, living with parents in Franklin, Erie Co, PA.
1920 Census, C.D. Culver, age 23, living with wife, Olive and son, George C., at Meadville, Ward 1, Crawford Co, PA.
1930 Census, Carl D. Culver, age 31, living with wife, Olive and children, at Meadville, West Mead Twp, Crawford Co, PA
1940 Census, Carl D. Culver, age 41, born in Pennsylvania, living on Elm Street, Warren, Trumbull Co, Ohio with a lady named Hazel Hawley age 29, born 1910-1911 in Ohio. Hazel is listed as being married and her previous residence (in 1935) was Akron, Summit Co, Ohio. Carl was listed as also married and a lodger at Hazel Hawley's residence. His last place of residence was Meadville, Crawford Co, PA. Olive's last place of residence was at Meadville, Crawford Co, Pennsylvania.

<table>
<tr><td>

NOTES FOR C. HAZEL CULVER:

Carl D. Culver married Hazel Clara Doerfer Hawley, daughter of John Wm. Doepher and Lana C. Young. She was born on April 16, 1910 in Pomeroy, Ohio and died on January 5, 1997 in Bradenton, Florida and she is buried beside Carl in the Manasota Memorial Cemetery. This is the same 'Hazel Hawley' from the 1940 Census. When they got married is unknown but Hazel changed her name on Social Security records on July 10, 1974 to 'Hazel Culver'. They had a son, Jerry V. Culver born 1942. Jerry lives in Bradenton today. Hazel was married previously [in 1930] to Clarence Hawley of Meigs Co, Ohio [1897-1971].

</td><td>

Social Security Record for:
Name: Hazel Culver
[Clara Hazel Doerfer]
SSN: 263573337
Gender: Female
Race: White
Birth Date: 16 Apr 1910
Birth Place: Pomeroy Meig, Ohio
Death Date: 5 Jan 1997
Father: John W Doerfer
Mother: Lana C Young
Type of Claim: Original SSN.
Notes: 10 Jul 1974: Name listed as HAZEL CULVER

</td></tr>
</table>

Children of Carl Culver and Olive DeRemer are:

      i. George C. Culver, born March 27, 1919 in Meadville, Crawford Co, Pennsylvania; died October 24, 2010 in Point Pleasant, West Virginia.

      ii. Mable G. Culver, born 1920 in Pennsylvania; died March 15, 2003 in Meadville, Crawford, PA; married Lipton.

2   iii. Leo Virgil Culver, born December 13, 1921 in Edinboro, Erie Co, Pennsylvania > Grove, Oklahoma; died March 04, 2010 in Grove, Delaware Co, Oklahoma >Olympus Cemetery; married (1) Helen Pearl McSparren Bef. 1941; married (2) Ione Jo Shampoe Abt. 1944 in Pennsylvania.

      iv. Leonard Owen Culver, born February 21, 1924 in Meadville, Crawford, Pennsylvania; died May 16, 2008 in Reno, Washoe, Nevada.

      v. Paul Culver, born 1926 in Pennsylvania; died 1926.

vi.   Carl D. Jr Culver, born August 04, 1927 in Meadville, Crawford, Pennsylvania; died April 07, 2000 in Tujunga, Los Angeles, California burial at Calvary Cemetery in Los Angeles.

vii.   James R. Culver, born 1930 in Pennsylvania.

viii.   Richard Culver, born 1930 in Pennsylvania.

ix.   Stanley Culver, born 1932 in Pennsylvania.

x.   Bernard Culver, born 1934 in Pennsylvania.

Child of Carl D. Culver & Hazel C. Doerfer:

i.   Jerry Vernon Culver born January 20, 1942 in Trumbull Co, Ohio. On August 7, 1981, in Ohio, he married Margaret M. Moraghan, the daughter of Stanley Novack and Mary David.

This man is Carl D. Culver Jr. born August 04, 1927 in Meadville, Crawford, Pennsylvania; died April 07, 2000 in Tujunga, Los Angeles, California, burial at Calvary Cemetery in Los Angeles.

6. *David William Sutton McSparren*, born November 29, 1884 in Bullion, Mineral Twp, Venango Co, Pennsylvania; and also lived in Rocky Grove, Venango, PA. He died May 10, 1972 in Franklin, Venango, PA and is buried at Hickory Grove Cemetery. He was the son of 12. George W. McSparren and 13. Rachel Carroll Sutton. David married 7. Annetta 'Nettie' Bell Umstead on January 17, 1906 in Franklin, Venango, PA.

7. *Annetta 'Nettie' Bell Umstead*, born January 25, 1891 in Pearl, Cranberry Twp, Venango Co, Pennsylvania and also of Rosary, Cranberry Twp, Venango, PA; she died January 06, 1953 in Franklin Hospital, Venango Co, PA. Nettie was the daughter of 14. Alfred Herstine Umstead and 15. Ida Frances Manross Bell.

Burial notes for David William Sutton McSparren:
Find A Grave Memorial# 123468696
Burial: Hickory Grove Cem, Victory Twp, Venango Co, PA

Burial notes for Annetta 'Nettie' Bell Umstead:
Find A Grave Memorial# 159269392

Children of David McSparren and Annetta Umstead are:

    i.   John David McSparren, born December 27, 1906 in Kennerdale, Venango Co, PA; died July 30, 1910 in Clinton Twp, Venango Co, PA >Hickory Grove Cemetery, died from Spinal Meningitis.

    ii.   George McSparren, born May 1908 in Franklin, Venango Co, PA; married Alberta Flockerzi; born 1910 in Oil City, PA.

    iii.   Pansy Irene McSparren, born August 05, 1909 in Washington Twp, Venango Co, PA.

    iv.   Frances Lydia McSparren, born August 24, 1908 in Franklin, Venango Co, PA; died June 28, 1957 in Ellwood City, Lawrence Co, PA; married Robert E. Spence; born Abt. 1907.

    v.   Blanche Freda McSparren, born July 13, 1912 in Franklin, Venango County, PA; died October 22, 2004 in Wampum, Lawrence Co, PA; married (1) Swartzfager Bef. 1930; married (2) George Albert Edwards Abt. 1931; born Abt. 1911.

    vi.   Lila G. McSparren, born 1915 in Venango County, PA.

3   vii.   Helen Pearl McSparren, born October 17, 1919 in Emlenton, Clariton Co, PA > Sugarcreek, Venango Co, Pennsylvania; died January 14, 1999 in Warren, Warren Co, Pennsylvania; married (1) Leo Virgil Culver Bef. 1941; married (2) Walker 1973.

    viii.   P. Clara McSparren, born 1920 in Venango Co, PA.

    ix.   A. George McSparren, born 1921 in Venango Co, PA.

    x.   William Ivan McSparren, born September 08, 1930 in Reno, Venango PA; died April 28, 2001 in Hartsville, South Carolina >Magnolia Cemetery. Military notes for William Ivan McSparren

Branch 1: ARMY Enlistment Date 1:   27 Jul 1948 Release Date 1:   10 Sep 1948

Mrs. Annetta Bell McSparren

Those attending funeral services for Mrs. David W. McSparren in the Burger Funeral Home on Thursday afternoon included Mr. and Mrs. Robert Spence, Ellwood City; Mr. and Mrs. George McSparren, of New Castle; Mrs. Blanche Edwards, Mrs. Cecelia Gravatt and William McSparren, all of Erie. Mr. and Mrs. Harry Umstead, of Van; Alfred Umstead, of Rockland; Lyle McSparren, of Coal Hill; Carl and David Umstead, both of Kennerdell.

Form V. S. No. 5.—50M.-3-25-09.

COMMONWEALTH OF PENNSYLVANIA.
BUREAU OF VITAL STATISTICS.
CERTIFICATE OF DEATH.

PLACE OF DEATH.

County of _Venango_

Township of _Clinton_

Registration District No. _870_

File No. _66062_

Borough of _______

Primary Registration District No. _3357_

Registered No. _______

City of _______ (No. _______ St.; _______ Ward)

[If death occurs away from USUAL RESIDENCE give facts called for under "Special Information."]

[If death occurred in a Hospital or Institution, give its NAME instead of street and number.]

FULL NAME _John McSparren_

PERSONAL AND STATISTICAL PARTICULARS	MEDICAL CERTIFICATE OF DEATH

SEX _Male_ | COLOR _White_

DATE OF BIRTH _Dec_ (Month) _27_ (Day) _1906_ (Year)

AGE _3_ years, _7_ months, _3_ days.

SINGLE, MARRIED, WIDOWED, OR DIVORCED _—_

BIRTHPLACE (State or Country) _Pa_

OCCUPATION _—_

NAME OF FATHER _David McSparren_

BIRTHPLACE OF FATHER (State or Country) _Pa_

MAIDEN NAME OF MOTHER _Annetta Umstead_

BIRTHPLACE OF MOTHER (State or Country) _Pa_

THE ABOVE STATED PERSONAL PARTICULARS ARE TRUE TO THE BEST OF MY KNOWLEDGE AND BELIEF

(Informant) _______

(Address) _______

Filed _Aug 8_ 1908 _______ Registrar

DATE OF DEATH _July_ (Month) _30_ (Day) _1908_ (Year)

I HEREBY CERTIFY, That I attended deceased from _July 28, 1908_ to _July 29 1908_ that I last saw h__ alive on _July 29 190__ and that death occurred, on the date stated above, at _4-30_ A. M. The CAUSE OF DEATH was as follows:

Spinal Meningitis

(Duration) _5_ Days

Contributory _______

(Duration) _______ Days

(Signed) _Geo. C. McGee_ M. D.

July 30 1908 (Address) _Wesley Pa_

SPECIAL INFORMATION only for Hospitals, Institutions, Transients, or Recent Residents.

Former or Usual Residence _______ How long at Place of Death _______ ?Days

Where was disease contracted? _______

PLACE OF BURIAL OR REMOVAL _Hickory Grove Cemetery_

DATE OF BURIAL _July 31_ 1908

UNDERTAKER _John Hutt_ ADDRESS _Clintonville Pa_

REGISTRATION CARD

SERIAL NUMBER 428   ORDER NUMBER 1933

1. David William McSparren
(First name) (Middle name) (Last name)

2. PERMANENT HOME ADDRESS:
1022½ Elm St., Franklin, Venango, Pa
(No.) (Street or R.F.D. No.) (City or town) (County) (State)

3. Age in Years: 33   4. Date of Birth: Nov. 29th. 1884
(Month) (Day) (Year)

RACE

White	Negro	Oriental	Indian	
			Citizen	Noncitizen
5 ✓	6	7	8	9

U. S. CITIZEN			ALIEN	
Native Born	Naturalized	Citizen by Father's Naturalization Before Registrant's Majority	Declarant	Non-declarant
10 ✓	11	12	13	14

15. If not a citizen of the U. S., of what nation are you a citizen or subject?

PRESENT OCCUPATION	EMPLOYER'S NAME
16 Ware-houseman	17 N. Y. C. R. R. Co.

18. PLACE OF EMPLOYMENT OR BUSINESS:
Elm St.   Franklin, Venango, Pa
(No.) (Street or R. F. D. No.) (City or town) (County) (State)

NEAREST RELATIVE
19 Name: Mrs. Annetta B. McSparren (wife)
20 Address: 1022½ Elm St., Franklin, Venango, Pa.
(No.) (Street or R.F.D. No.) (City or town) (County) (State)

I AFFIRM THAT I HAVE VERIFIED ABOVE ANSWERS AND THAT THEY ARE TRUE

P. M. G. O.   David William McSparren
Form No. 1 (Red)   (Registrant's signature or mark)   (OVER)

REGISTRAR'S REPORT   37-2-31. C

DESCRIPTION OF REGISTRANT

HEIGHT			BUILD			COLOR OF EYES	COLOR OF HAIR
Tall	Medium	Short	Slender	Medium	Stout		
21	22	23	24 ✓	25	26	27 Dark Brown	28 Dark Brown

29. Has person lost arm, leg, hand, eye, or is he obviously physically disqualified? (Specify.)

None

30. I certify that my answers are true; that the person registered has read or has had read to him his own answers; that I have witnessed his signature or mark, and that all of his answers of which I have knowledge are true, **except as follows:**

Elizabeth Surgers
(Signature of Registrar)

Date of Registration Sept. 12, 1918

Local Board for Division No. 1
for the
County of Venango, State of Penna.
(STAMP OF LOCAL BOARD)

(The stamp of the Local Board having jurisdiction of the area in which the registrant has his permanent home shall be placed in this box.)

63—6171   (OVER)

REGISTRATION CARD—(Men born on or after April 28, 1877 and on or before February 16, 1897)

SERIAL NUMBER U929   1. NAME (Print) David William McSparren   ORDER NUMBER
(First) (Middle) (Last)

2. PLACE OF RESIDENCE (Print)
Richland, Venango, Penna.
(Number and street) (Town, township, village, etc.) (County) (State)
[THE PLACE OF RESIDENCE GIVEN ON THE LINE ABOVE WILL DETERMINE LOCAL BOARD JURISDICTION; LINE 2 OF REGISTRATION CERTIFICATE WILL BE IDENTICAL]

3. MAILING ADDRESS
R.D. #1, Emlenton, Penna.
(Mailing address if other than place indicated on line 2. If same insert word same)

4. TELEPHONE —   5. AGE IN YEARS 58   6. PLACE OF BIRTH Mineral Twp, Venango Co.
(Town or county)
DATE OF BIRTH November 29, 1884   Pennsylvania
(Exchange) (Number) (Mo) (Day) (Yr) (State or country)

7. NAME AND ADDRESS OF PERSON WHO WILL ALWAYS KNOW YOUR ADDRESS
Mrs. Minnie Oesau, 1117 Chestnut St., Franklin Pa

8. EMPLOYER'S NAME AND ADDRESS
Joy Manufacturing Co., Franklin, Penna.

9. PLACE OF EMPLOYMENT OR BUSINESS
Franklin, Venango, Penna.
(Number and street or R. F. D. number) (Town) (County) (State)

I AFFIRM THAT I HAVE VERIFIED ABOVE ANSWERS AND THAT THEY ARE TRUE.

D. S. S. Form 1
(Revised 4-1-42)   (over)   16-21630-1   David W. McSparren
(Registrant's signature)

REGISTRAR'S REPORT

DESCRIPTION OF REGISTRANT

RACE		HEIGHT (Approx.)	WEIGHT (Approx.)	COMPLEXION	
White	✓	5'9½"	165	Sallow	
		EYES	HAIR	Light	✓
Negro		Blue ✓	Blonde	Ruddy	
		Gray	Red	Dark	
Oriental		Hazel	Brown	Freckled	
		Brown	Black	Light brown	
Indian		Black	Gray	Dark brown	
			Bald ✓	Black	
Filipino					

Other obvious physical characteristics that will aid in identification

One Glass eye (right) & rupture

I certify that my answers are true; that the person registered has read or has had read to him his own answers; that I have witnessed his signature or mark and that all of his answers of which I have knowledge are true, except as follows:

Mrs. Esther B. Cramer
(Signature of registrar)

Registrar for Local Board _____ 1 _____ Venango _____ Pa. _____
(Number)   (City or county)   (State)

Date of registration _____ 4/27/42 _____

PLACE OF BIRTH   COMMONWEALTH OF PENNSYLVANIA
Bureau of Vital Statistics
CERTIFICATE OF BIRTH   160844

County of _Venango_
Township of _Clinton_
or
Borough of ________
or
City of ________
No. ________, ________ St.   Registration District No. _870_   File No. ________
Primary Registration District No. _9357_   Registered No. _26_
________ Ward.

FULL NAME OF CHILD _John David McSparren_

| Sex of Child _female_ | Twin, Triplet, or other? _single_ | and | Number in order of birth _—_ | Legitimate? _yes_ | Date of birth _Dec 27th_ 190_6_ (Month) (Day) (Year) |

	FATHER		MOTHER
FULL NAME	_David McSparren_	FULL MAIDEN NAME	_Annetta Umstead_
RESIDENCE	_Kennerdel Pa_	RESIDENCE	_Kennerdel Pa_
COLOR	_White_ AGE AT LAST BIRTHDAY _22_ (Years)	COLOR	_White_ AGE AT LAST BIRTHDAY _16_ (Years)
BIRTHPLACE	_Pearl Pa_	BIRTHPLACE	_Oil City Pa_
OCCUPATION	_Laborer_	OCCUPATION	_housewife_

Number of child of this mother _first_   Number of children, of this mother, now living _one_

CERTIFICATE OF ATTENDING PHYSICIAN OR MIDWIFE*

I hereby certify that I attended the birth of this child, and that it occurred on _Dec 27th_, 190_6_, at _8_ _a._ M.

*When there was no attending physician or midwife, then the father, mother, householder, etc., should make this return.

(Signature) ________________
Clintonville
(Physician or Midwife)

Given name added from a supplemental report
Dec 28 ________, 190_6_
________ Registrar

Address ________
Filed ________, 190_ ________ Registrar

PLACE OF BIRTH   COMMONWEALTH OF PENNSYLVANIA
Bureau of Vital Statistics
CERTIFICATE OF BIRTH

County of _Butler_
Township of _Washington_
or
Borough of ________
or
City of ________
No. ________, ________ St.

104737   Registration District No. _54_   File No. _99_
Primary Registration District No. _2275_   Registered No. ________
________ Ward.

FULL NAME OF CHILD _Pansy Irene McSparren_

| Sex of Child _Female_ | Twin, Triplet, or other? | and | Number in order of birth | Legitimate? _yes_ | Date of birth _Aug 25_, 190_8_ (Month) (Day) (Year) |

	FATHER		MOTHER
FULL NAME	_David W. McSparren_	FULL MAIDEN NAME	_nette Umstead_
RESIDENCE	_Washington Township_	RESIDENCE	_Washington T.P._
COLOR	_White_ AGE AT LAST BIRTHDAY _23_ (Years)	COLOR	_White_ AGE AT LAST BIRTHDAY _17_ (Years)
BIRTHPLACE	_Venango Co._	BIRTHPLACE	_Venango Co._
OCCUPATION	_Laborer_	OCCUPATION	_Wife_

Number of child of this mother _2 nd_   Number of children, of this mother, now living _two_

CERTIFICATE OF ATTENDING PHYSICIAN OR MIDWIFE*

I hereby certify that I attended the birth of this child, and that it occurred on _Aug 25_, 190_8_, at _11:30 A_ M.

*When there was no attending physician or midwife, then the father, mother, householder, etc., should make this return.

(Signature) _O P Pisor_
Physician
(Physician or Midwife)

Given name added from a supplemental report
________, 190_

Address _No Hope, Pa._
Filed _Aug 28_, 190_8_   _O P Pisor_ Registrar

HVS-20143—525M—9-55 ◆—10

COMMONWEALTH OF PENNSYLVANIA
DEPARTMENT OF HEALTH
DIVISION OF VITAL STATISTICS

File No. **53661**

Primary Dist. No. **371-357**

CERTIFICATE OF DEATH

Registered No. **100**

1. PLACE OF DEATH
a. County **Lawrence**
b. City, Borough or Township **Ellwood City**
c. Length of stay in 1b. **15 years**
d. FULL NAME (If NOT in hospital, give street address) of HOSPITAL or INSTITUTION **Ellwood City Hospital**
e. Is Place of Death Inside Municipality Limits? Yes ☒ No ☐   **20**

2. USUAL RESIDENCE (where deceased lived. If institution: residence before admission)
a. State **Penna.**
b. County **Lawrence**
c. City, Borough or Township **Ellwood City**   **371**
d. Street Address or Location **500 Highland Avenue**
e. Is Residence Inside Municipality Limits? Yes ☒ No ☐   f. Is Residence on a Farm? Yes ☐ No ☒

3. NAME OF DECEASED (Type or print)
a. (First) **FRANCES**   b. (Middle) **LYDA**   c. (Last) **SPENCE**

4. DATE OF DEATH (Month) (Day) (Year) **June 28, 1957**

5. SEX **Female**   **6. COLOR OR RACE** **White**
7. MARRIED ☒ NEVER MARRIED ☐ WIDOWED ☐ DIVORCED ☐
8. DATE OF BIRTH **8-24-1908**
9. AGE (in years last birthday) **48** — If under 1 year: Months / Days — If under 24 hrs.: Hours / Min.

10. FULL NAME OF SPOUSE **Robert E. Spence**
11. BIRTHPLACE (Also give state or foreign country) **Franklin, Penna.**
12. CITIZEN OF WHAT COUNTRY **U.S.A.**

13. FATHER'S NAME **David McSparren**
14. MOTHER'S MAIDEN NAME **Annetta Umbstead**

15. USUAL OCCUPATION (even if retired) **Housewife-Own Home**
16. Social Security No. **none**
17. INFORMANT **Robert E Spence-Ellwood City, Penna** ADDRESS **500 Highland Ave**

MEDICAL CERTIFICATION

18. CAUSE OF DEATH [Enter only one cause per line for (a), (b) & (c)]

PART 1. Death was caused by:
IMMEDIATE CAUSE (a) *Coronary Occlusion*

Conditions, if any, which gave rise to above cause (a) stating the underlying cause last.
DUE TO (b) *Coron. Sclerosis*
DUE TO (c)

INTERVAL BETWEEN ONSET AND DEATH
Instant
2 years
4201

PART II. OTHER SIGNIFICANT CONDITIONS [contributing to death but not related to the terminal disease given in Part I (a)]

19. WAS AUTOPSY PERFORMED? Yes ☐ No ☒

20a. ACCIDENT ☐ SUICIDE ☐ HOMICIDE ☐
20b. DESCRIBE HOW INJURY OCCURRED.
20c. Time of Injury Hour, m. E.S.T. — Month, Day, Year

20d. INJURY OCCURRED While at work ☐ Not while at work ☐
20e. PLACE OF INJURY (e.g., home, farm, factory, street, etc.)
20f. CITY, BOROUGH, TOWNSHIP — COUNTY — STATE

21. I hereby certify that I attended the deceased from *Jan. 18*, 1955 to *June 28*, 1957, that I last saw the deceased alive on *June 27*, 1957, and that death occurred at **3:55** Am., E.S.T., from the causes and on the date stated above.

22a. SIGNATURE *J C Painter*, M.D. or D.O. , M.D.
22b. ADDRESS **80 Pgh. Circle Ellwood City, Penna.**
22c. DATE SIGNED **6-28-1957**

23a. BURIAL ☒ CREMATION ☐ REMOVAL ☐
23b. DATE **7-1-57**
23c. NAME OF CEMETERY OR CREMATORY **Locust Grove Cemetery**
23d. LOCATION (City, Boro, Twp. & County) (State) **North Sewickley Twp. Beaver County - Penna.**

24. DATE REC'D BY REG. **6-30-57**
25. REGISTRAR'S SIGNATURE *Mrs. Thomas Beatrice*
26. SIGNATURE OF FUNERAL DIRECTOR *Kenneth C. Timm* ADDRESS **Ellwood City, Pa.**
Patton Memorial Home

11-15-29-40,000 (17-3102)

Notice to Town and City Clerks. This form is to be used only by town and city clerks for making copies of marriage records to be filed with county clerks. It must not be given to applicants for marriage licenses or used by clergymen or magistrates for the certification of a marriage.

PLACE OF REGISTRY
STATE OF NEW YORK

NEW YORK STATE DEPARTMENT OF HEALTH

Division of Vital Statistics

County of Niagra

MARRIAGE LICENSE

Registered No. 6

Town or City Lewiston

Know all Men by this Certificate, that any person authorized by law to perform marriage ceremonies within the state of New York to whom this may come, he, not knowing any lawful impediment thereto, is hereby authorized and empowered to solemnize the rites of matrimony between George Mc Sparren of Oil City Penn in the county of Venorgo and state of New York and Albert Flockerzi of Venorgo Oil City, penn in the county of and state of New York and to certify the same to be said parties or either of them under his hand and seal in his ministerial or official capacity and thereupon he is required to return his certificate in the form hereto annexed. The statements endorsed hereon or annexed hereto, by me subscribed, contain a full and true abstract of all the facts concerning such parties disclosed by their affidavits or verified statements presented to me upon the application for this license.

In Testimony Whereof, I have hereunto set my hand and affixed the seal of said Town or City at Lewiston this Twenty-Seventh day of Frebruary nineteen hundred and Thirty

{ SEAL }

Florebce H. Lum

Town

Clerk

The following is a full and true abstract of all the facts disclosed by the above-named applicants in their verified statements presented to me upon their applications for the above license:

FROM THE GROOM	FROM THE BRIDE
Full name George Mc Sparren	Full name Albert Flockerzi
Color White	Color White
Place of residence Oil City (street address)	Place of residence Oil City (street address)
Venango (city, town or village) Pa. (state)	Venorgo (city, town or village) Penn (state)
Age 21 Date of birth May 1908	Age 21 Date of birth 1910
Occupation Laborer	Occupation Stenographer
Place of birth Franklin, Pa.	Place of birth Oil City
Name of groom's father David W. Mc Sparren	Name of bride's father Agam Flockerzi
Country of father's birth Bullion, Pa.	Country of father's birth Oil City Pa.
Maiden name of groom's mother Anne Lee Umstead	Maiden name of bride's mother Emma Johnson
Country of mother's birth Pearl, Pa.	Country of mother's birth Oil City Pa.
Number of proposed marriage First	Number of proposed marriage First
I have not to my knowledge been infected with any venereal disease, or if I have been so infected within five years I have had a laboratory test within that period which shows that I am now free from infection from any such disease.	I have not to my knowledge been infected with any venereal disease, or if I have been so infected within five years I have had a laboratory test within that period which shows that I am now free from infection from any such disease.
Former wife or wives living or dead None	Former husband or husbands living or dead None
Is applicant a divorced person No	Is applicant a divorced person No
If so, when and where, and against whom divorce or divorces were granted	If so, when and where, and against whom divorce or divorces were granted
I declare that no legal impediment exists as to my right to enter into the marriage state.	I declare that no legal impediment exists as to my right to enter into the marriage state.

COUNTY CLERK COPY

FUTURE ADDRESS (Enter here EXACT FUTURE ADDRESS after marriage if known)

Erie Pa.

(street address)　　　　　(city, town or village)　　　　　(state)

(Great Grandparents)
Found: 8 of 8

8. *Carson Earl Culver*, born October 21, 1877 in Edinboro, Erie Co, Pennsylvania, also lived in Franklin, Erie Co, PA. He died December 2, 1948 at Capitol Heights, Prince George's County, Maryland and is buried in the Cedar Hill Cemetery at Suitland, MD. He was the son of 16. Matthias Lyrus Culver and 17. Marilla "Rillie" E. Davison. He married 9. Mabel Mae Holt July 26, 1898 in Washington Twp, Erie County, Pennsylvania.

9. *Mabel Mae Holt*, born May 30, 1879 in Leavitt, Oceana County, Michigan and relocated with her parents to Oakland Twp, Venango Co, Pennsylvania. Mabel and her husband relocated to Capital Heights, Prince George's Co, Maryland before 1940, where she died on January 14, 1942; burial in Cedar Hill Cemetery. She was the daughter of 18. Eli Mark Holt and 19. Isabelle H. 'Belle' Wicks.

CULVER, CARSON E. On Thursday, December 2, 1948, at Reverend Optis home Catonsville, Md, CARSON E CULVER husband of the late Mabel M Culver, the beloved father of Carl, Clyde, Claude, Clair, Choice Culver, Hazel Compton, Ilda Gateau, Autumn Smith, Thelma Rice, and Lucille Bartz. Services at Chambers Funeral Home, 517 11th St. se, on Saturday December 4, at 2:30 p.m. Interment Cedar Hill Cemetery

Above: Death Notice for Carson E. Culver "The Washington Post" January 17, 1942
"On Thursday, December 2, 1948 at Reverend Optois home Catonsville, Md, Carson E. Culver husband of the late Mabel M. Culver, the beloved father of Carl Clyde, Claude, Clair, Choce Culver, Hazel Compton, Ilda Gateau, Autumn Smith, Thelma Rice and Lucille Bartz. Services at Chambers Funeral Home 517 11th St. SE, on Saturday December 4, at 2:30 p.m. Interment Cedar Hill Cemetery."

Burial notes for Carson Earl Culver:
Find A Grave Memorial# 180850421

Burial notes for Mabel Holt Culver:
Find A Grave Memorial# 180850340

CULVER, MABEL. On Wednesday, January 14, 1942, at Casualty Hospital, MABEL CULVER, beloved wife of Carson E. Culver and mother of ten children. She is also survived by one sister and two brothers. Funeral services will be held at her sons's residence, 204 Avenue D, District Heights, Md., on Saturday, January 17, at 1 p. m. Relatives and friends invited to attend. Interment Cedar Hill Cemetery.

1880 Census, Carson Culver, age 3, living in Richmond Twp, Crawford Co, PA with father, Mathias, mother Murilla and grandparents, Joseph & Sarah Culver, and his brother Carl and two sisters, Cherie & Ellen.
1900 Census, Carson E. Culver age 23, living in Oakland Twp, Venango Co, PA with wife Mabel age 21; Carrol D. (Carl D) age 2; Claude M. & Clyde E., twins age one.
1907 City Directory, Culver, Carson, farmer Elk Creek Twp. Erie Co, PA.
1910 Census, Carson E. Culver, age 32, living in Franklin Twp, Erie Co, PA with 5 children and wife Mabel.
1920 Census, Carson & Mabel Culver living in Washington Twp, Erie Co, PA; children Hazel, Choice, Ida, Autumn, Thelma.
1930 Census, Carson E. & Mabel M. Culver are living at Greater Capitol Heights, Prince George's Co, Maryland. Others in household: Choice H.; Autumn; Thelma; Lucille; Clyde E.; Helen D.; William H. Gateau (son in law) and Ilda R.
1940 Census, Carson & Mabel Culver living at Greater Capitol Heights (Hillside) Prince George's, Maryland with daughter Lucille age 17 born in PA (1923). Carson's occupation listed as a Contractor - Paper Hanger.

Children of Carson Culver and Mabel Holt are:

4   i. Carl Dewey Culver, born June 22, 1898 in Venango County, PA> West Mead Twp, Crawford Co, Pennsylvania; died September 12, 1993 in Manatee Co, Florida>Manasota Memorial Park Cemetery at Bradenton, FL; married (1) Olive Madeline DeRemer June 15, 1918 in Meadville, PA; married (2) Clara Hazel Doerfer 1974.

     ii. Claude M. Culver, born December 1899 in Oakland Twp, Venango Co, PA; died 1982.

    iii. Clyde E. Culver, born December 1899 in Oakland Twp, Venango Co, PA; died 1964.

iv. Clair R. Culver, born 1901 in Oakland Twp, Venango Co, PA; died 1973.

v. Hazel B. Culver, born 1904 in Venango County, PA.

vi. Choice H. Culver, born June 21, 1911 in Edinboro, Erie Co, Pennsylvania; died February 14, 2003 in LaPlata, Charles Co, Maryland >Trinity Memorial Gardens Cemetery at Waldorf, Maryland; married Hester Rollins; born Abt. 1912.

Notes for Choice H. Culver:

Find A Grave Memorial# 7208451

vii. Ida R. Culver, born 1913 in Pennsylvania; died 2005; married William H. Gateau; born 1912 in District of Columbia.

viii. Autumn Culver, born 1915 in Pennsylvania.

ix. Thelma Culver, born 1920 in Pennsylvania; died 2000.

x. Lucille Algena Culver, born September 09, 1922 in Edinboro, Erie Co, Pennsylvania; died February 29, 1996 in 20601 Waldorf, Charles Co, Maryland; married Herman Bartz; born Abt. 1921.

REGISTRATION CARD

SERIAL NUMBER 766 — ORDER NUMBER 102

1 Carson Earl Culver

2 PERMANENT HOME ADDRESS: R.D.3 Edinboro Erie Pa

3 Age in Years 40 — 4 Date of Birth Oct 21 1877

RACE — White ✓

U. S. CITIZEN — Native Born ✓

16 PRESENT OCCUPATION: Farmer

18 PLACE OF EMPLOYMENT OR BUSINESS: R.D 3 Edinboro Erie Pa

NEAREST RELATIVE Name: Mrs Mabel Culver
Address: Rd 3 Edinboro Erie Pa

I AFFIRM THAT I HAVE VERIFIED ABOVE ANSWERS AND THAT THEY ARE TRUE

P. M. G. O. Form No. 1 (Red) — Carson E Culver (OVER)

REGISTRAR'S REPORT

DESCRIPTION OF REGISTRANT

HEIGHT			BUILD			COLOR OF EYES	COLOR OF HAIR
Tall	Medium	Short	Slender	Medium	Stout		
21	22 ✓	23	24	25 ✓	26	27 Blue	28 Light

29 Has person lost arm, leg, hand, eye, or is he obviously physically disqualified? (Specify.)

30 I certify that my answers are true; that the person registered has read or has had read to him his own answers; that I have witnessed his signature or mark, and that all of his answers of which I have knowledge are true, except as follows:

M. D. Gehr
(Signature of Registrar)

Date of Registration Sept 12 1918

LOCAL BOARD No. 2

(STAMP OF LOCAL BOARD)

(The stamp of the Local Board having jurisdiction of the area in which the registrant has his permanent home shall be placed in this box.) (OVER)

MARRIAGE LICENSE DOCKET.

Mr Carson E Culver

— TO —

Miss Mable M Holt

Marriage License No. 7343

On this 26th day of July A. D. 1898, appeared Mr. Carson E Culver and applied for license for the marriage of Mr. Carson E Culver , a resident of the town of Washington County of Erie , State of Penn^a , aged 21 years, to Miss Mable M Holt , a resident of the town of Washington County of Erie , State of Penn^a , aged 19 years. Same day affidavit required by act of Assembly made before Clerk of Court

and filed, establishing the legality of the said contemplated marriage; and it appearing that there is no legal impediment thereto, a marriage license in due form was issued authorizing any Minister of the Gospel, Justice of the Peace, or other person authorized by law to solemnize marriages, to join said Mr Carson E Culver and Miss Mable M Holt together in the Holy State of Matrimony.

And the said Mr. and Miss Mable M Holt being a minor the consent of Eli M Holt the father

of the said minor to the contemplated marriage was first given before said Clerk personally (by proper legal certificate filed and duly signed, attested and acknowledged).

Now this twenty-seventh day of July , A. D. 1898, there was received and filed here certificate as follows, to-wit :

"I hereby certify, that on the twenty-sixth day of July A. D. one thousand eight hundred and ninety-eight at Erie Pa Mr. Carson E Culver and Miss Mable M Holt were by me united in marriage in accordance with license issued by the Clerk of Orphans' Court of Erie County, Pennsylvania, numbered 7343 "

Jacob E. Swan
(Minister of the Gospel.)
(Justice of the Peace.)
Alderman

Attest :

James H Allison Clerk Orphans' Court.

10. *George William DeRemer*, born May 01, 1869 in Guys Mills, Crawford Co, PA; he died November 04, 1945 in Meadville, Crawford Co, Pennsylvania and is buried at Blooming Valley Cemetery. He was the son of 20. Levi DeRemer and 21. Irene Heath. He married 11. Minnie Mae Clark on March 06, 1893 in Pennsylvania. He married 2nd, Eleanor Lillian Manross.

11. *Minnie Mae Clark*, born September 29, 1877 in Blooming Valley, Crawford Co, PA; she died May 05, 1917 in Meadville, Crawford Co, Pennsylvania and is buried at ____________ Cemetery. She was the daughter of 22. Jacob C. Clark and 23. Jenny Mae Coy.

Children of George DeRemer and Minnie Clark are:

      i.   Son DeRemer, born 1894 in Crawford Co, PA; died 1894 in Crawford Co, PA.

     ii.   Fred Joseph DeRemer, born 1897 in Crawford Co, PA; died 1969.

5   iii.   **Olive Madeline DeRemer**, born January 16, 1899 in Blooming Valley, Crawford Co, PA; died February 05, 1975 in Meadville, Crawford Co, PA, burial at Blooming Valley Cemetery; she married **Carl Dewey Culver** June 15, 1918 in Meadville, PA.

     iv.   Harold DeRemer, born 1901 in Crawford Co, PA; died 1932.

     v.   Jacob DeRemer, born 1902 in Crawford Co, PA; died 1981.

     vi.   Pearl Frances DeRemer, born 1908 in Crawford Co, PA; died 1994.

HVS-20010—150M—7-43

COMMONWEALTH OF PENNSYLVANIA
DEPARTMENT OF HEALTH
BUREAU OF VITAL STATISTICS

File No. 93812

Primary Dist. No. 20-07-01

CERTIFICATE OF DEATH

656

Registered No. 346

---

1. PLACE OF DEATH:
(a) County Crawford
(b) Township
(c) Borough
(d) City Meadville
(e) Name of hospital or institution City Hospital
(If not in hospital or inst. write street number or location)
(f) Length of stay: In hospital or inst. 3 wks (g) In this community

2. USUAL RESIDENCE OF DECEASED:
(a) State Pa. (b) County Crawford
(c) City or town Guys Mills
(If outside city or town limits, write RURAL)
(d) Street No. R.1.
(If rural give location)
(e) If citizen of foreign country, name country

---

3. (a) FULL NAME George W. DeRemer

3. (b) If U.S. Veteran, complete reverse side of certificate
3. (c) Social Security No.

4. Sex M race W
5. Color or race W
6. (a) Single, widowed, married, divorced W

6. (b) Name of husband or wife innie Clark DeRemer
6. (c) Age of husband or wife if alive ____ years

7. Birth date of deceased May 1, 1869
(Month) (Day) (Year)

8. AGE: Years	Months	Days	If less than one day	
76	6	3	hr.	min.

9. Birthplace RFD Guys Mills, Pa.
(City, town, or county) (State or foreign country)
10. Usual occupation Farming
11. Industry or business Own farm

MOTHER FATHER
12. Name Levi DeRemer
13. Birthplace (Unknown)
(City, town, or county) (State or foreign country)
14. Maiden name Irene Heth
15. Birthplace (Unknown)
(City, town, or county) (State or foreign country)

16. (a) Informant's own signature ____
(b) Address R.1, Guys Mills, Pa.

17. (a) Burial (b) Date thereof Nov. 7, 1945
(Burial, cremation, or removal) (Month) (Day) (Year)
(c) Place Blooming Valley Cem County Crawford State Pa.

18. (a) Signature of funeral director ____
(b) Address Meadville, Pa.

19. (a) Nov. 6, 1945 (b) ____
(Date received loc'l registrar) (Registrar's signature)

MEDICAL CERTIFICATION

20. Date of death: Month NOV. day 4
year 1945 hour 11 minute 50 AM

21. I hereby certify that I attended the deceased from 10/13/45
, 19 , to 11/4/45 , 19
that I last saw him alive on 11/4 , 19 45
and that death occurred on the date and hour stated above.

Immediate cause of death
Chronic Myocarditis

DURATION
2-3 yrs

Due to
124#

Due to
93#

Other conditions
(Include pregnancy within 3 months of death)
Cirrhosis of Liver.

Major findings:
Of operations

PHYSICIAN
Underline the cause to which death should be charged statistically.

Of autopsy

22. If death was due to external causes, fill in the following:
(a) (Probably) Accident, suicide, or homicide (specify)
(b) Date of occurrence
(c) Where did injury occur?
(City or town) (County) (State)
(d) Did injury occur in or about home, on farm, in industrial place, in public place?
(Specify type of place)
While at work (e) Means of injury

Signature ____ (M. D. or other)
Address Meadville Pa. Date signed 11/5/45

Form V. S. No. 5—50M.-4-12-12.

CERTIFICATE OF DEATH.

COMMONWEALTH OF PENNSYLVANIA.
DEPARTMENT OF HEALTH
BUREAU OF VITAL STATISTICS

1. **PLACE OF DEATH**

County of *Crawford*
Township of ....
or Borough of ....
or City of *Meadville* (No. .... St. .... Ward.)

Registration District No. *435*
Primary Registration District No. *114*

File No. *54814*
Registered No. *113*

[If death occurred in a Hospital or Institution, give its NAME instead of street and number.]

2. **FULL NAME** *Minnie De Remer*

PERSONAL AND STATISTICAL PARTICULARS	MEDICAL CERTIFICATE OF DEATH

3. SEX *Female* 4. COLOR OR RACE *White* 5. SINGLE, MARRIED, WIDOWED OR DIVORCED (Write the word.) *Married*

16. DATE OF DEATH *May 5 1917* (Month) (Day) (Year)

6. DATE OF BIRTH *Sept* (Month) *29* (Day) *1877* (Year)

17. *Apr 29" 191.7* to *May 5" 191.7* I HEREBY CERTIFY, That I attended deceased from that I last saw h__ alive on *May 5 191.7* and that death occurred, on the date stated above, at *1* P.M. M.

7. AGE *39* yrs. *7* mos. *6* ds. If LESS than 1 day how many ......hrs. or ......min.?

The CAUSE OF DEATH* was as follows: *Acute Peritonitis not puerperal*
(Duration) ......yrs. ......mos. *6* ds

8. OCCUPATION
(a) Trade, profession, or particular kind of work *Housewife*
(b) General nature of industry, business, or establishment in which employed (or employer) ....

112

Contributory (SECONDARY) ....
(Duration) ......yrs. ......mos. ......ds.

9. BIRTHPLACE (State or Country) *Pennsylvania*

PARENTS
10. NAME OF FATHER *Jacob Clark.*
11. BIRTHPLACE OF FATHER (State or Country) *Pennsylvania*

(Signed) *W D Hanshen* M.D.
May 7 1917 (Address) *Meadville, Pa*

12. MAIDEN NAME OF MOTHER *Jennie Coy.*
13. BIRTHPLACE OF MOTHER (State or Country) *Pennsylvania*

*State the DISEASE CAUSING DEATH; or in deaths from VIOLENT CAUSES, state (1) MEANS OF INJURY; and (2) whether ACCIDENTAL, SUICIDAL, OR HOMICIDAL.

14. THE ABOVE IS TRUE TO THE BEST OF MY KNOWLEDGE.
(Informant) *G. W. De Remer*
(Address) *Guys Mills, Pa.*

18. LENGTH OF RESIDENCE (FOR HOSPITALS, INSTITUTIONS, TRANSIENTS OR RECENT RESIDENTS).
At place of death ......yrs. *6* mos. ......ds. In the State ......yrs. ......mos. ......ds.
Where was disease contracted, if not at place of death? *near Guys Mills Pa*
Former or usual residence *near Guys Mills Pa*

15.
Filed *5-8 191.7* .... Local Registrar

19. PLACE OF BURIAL OR REMOVAL *Blooming Valley, Pa.* DATE OF BURIAL *May 8 1917* 191...
20. UNDERTAKER *Willard C. Waid* ADDRESS *Guys Mills, Pa.*

---

12.   George W. McSparren, born October 19, 1845 in Venango Co, PA; died September 03, 1926 in Sugarcreek, Venango, PA >Hickory Grove Cemetery in Polk, PA. He was the son of 24. Robert McSparren and 25. Nancy_________. George married 13. Rachel Carroll Sutton Bef. 1867 in Pennsylvania.

13.   Rachel Carroll Sutton, born June 23, 1844 in Irwin, Venango Co, PA; died December 02, 1929 in Venango Co, PA > Hickory Grove Cemetery. She was the daughter of 26. Reuben Sutton and 27. Elizabeth 'Eliza' Ann Alcorn.

Notes for George W. McSparren:
George states on the 1910 Census that his father was born in Scotland but think that is wrong as Robert McSparren states that he was born in Pennsylvania.
Find A Grave Memorial# 69737695
Burial: Hickory Grove Cem, Victory Twp, Venango Co, PA

Notes for Rachel Carroll Sutton:
Find A Grave Memorial# 69737721
Burial: Hickory Grove Cem, Victory Twp, Venango Co, PA

Children of George McSparren and Rachel Sutton are:

    i.   Minnie Jane McSparren, born 1867; died 1946; married John Lincoln Oesan October 18, 1893 in Franklin, Venango, PA; born Abt. 1866.

    ii.   Mary Ann McSparren, born February 1870 in Franklin, Venango, PA; died 1887 in Franklin, Venango, PA >Hickory Grove Cemetery; married Thomas Stevenson; born Abt. 1870.

    iii.   Charles Harvey McSparren, born February 15, 1874 in Venango Co, PA; died September 14, 1944 in Franklin, Venango, PA >Hickory Grove Cemetery.

    iv.   Ambrose W. McSparren, born 1880 in Venango Co, PA.

6   v.   David William Sutton McSparren, born November 29, 1884 in Bullion, Mineral Twp, Venango Co, PA> of Rocky Grove, Venango, PA; died May 10, 1972 in Franklin, Venango, PA>Hickory Grove Cemetery; married Annetta 'Nettie' Bell Umstead January 17, 1906 in Franklin, Venango, PA.

    vi.   Benjamin W. McSparren, born 1878 in Franklin, Venango Co, PA; married Bertha M. Carter November 05, 1902; born 1885 in Sugar Creek, PA.

    vii.   Lyda Ellen McSparren, born October 11, 1873 in Franklin, Venango Co, PA; died August 20, 1935 in Franklin, Venango Co, PA; married Charles L. Brakeman; born Abt. 1871.

CERTIFICATE OF DEATH

COMMONWEALTH OF PENNSYLVANIA
DEPARTMENT OF HEALTH
BUREAU OF VITAL STATISTICS

625

File No. 74519

N. B.—Every item of information should be carefully supplied. AGE should be stated EXACTLY. PHYSICIANS should state CAUSE OF DEATH in plain terms, so that it may be properly classified. Exact Statement of OCCUPATION is very important. See instructions on back of certificate.

WRITE PLAINLY WITH UNFADING INK—THIS IS A PERMANENT RECORD

1. PLACE OF DEATH

County of *Venango*

Township of

or Borough of

or City of *Franklin*

Registration District No. ....

Primary Registration District No. 61-04-01

Registered No. 220

[If death occurred in a Hospital or Institution give its NAME instead of street and number.]

2. FULL NAME *Mrs. Lyda Ellen Brakeman*

(a) Residence, No. *217 Elk St.* St., ... Ward. ....
(Usual Place of Abode)

Length of residence in city or town where death occurred yrs. mos. ds. How long in U. S., if of foreign birth? yrs. mos. ds.

(If nonresident give city or town and State)

PERSONAL AND STATISTICAL PARTICULARS

3. SEX *F*

4. COLOR OR RACE *W.*

5. SINGLE, MARRIED, WIDOWED OR DIVORCED (write the word) *Married*

5a. If married, widowed, or divorced HUSBAND of (or) WIFE of *Charles L. Brakeman*

6. DATE OF BIRTH (month, day and year) *Oct. 11, 1873*

7. AGE Years *61* Months *10* Days *9* — IF LESS than 1 day ...... hrs. or ...... min.

8. OCCUPATION OF DECEASED
(a) Trade, profession, or particular kind of work *Housewife*
(b) General nature of industry, business or establishment in which employed (or employer)
(c) Name of employer

9. BIRTHPLACE (city or town) (State or Country) *Pa.*

10. NAME OF FATHER *George McSparren*

11. BIRTHPLACE OF FATHER (city or town) (State or Country) *Pa.*

12. MAIDEN NAME OF MOTHER *Rachael Sutton*

13. BIRTHPLACE OF MOTHER (city or town) (State or Country) *Pa.*

14. Informant *C. L. Brakeman*
(Address) *Franklin Pa.*

15. Filed *Aug., 21,,* 1935 *Mary M. Orlando* Registrar

MEDICAL CERTIFICATE OF DEATH

16. DATE OF DEATH *August 20,* 1935
(Month) (Day) (Year)

17. I HEREBY CERTIFY, That I attended deceased from *April 8,* 1934 to *Aug. 20,* 1935, that I last saw her alive on *Aug. 19,* 1935, and that death occurred, on the date stated above, at *1:45 A.* m.

The CAUSE OF DEATH* was as follows:
Chronic myocarditis with decompensation

...... (duration) ...... yrs., ... mos. ...... days

CONTRIBUTORY (Secondary) ......
...... (duration) ...... yrs. ...... mos. ...... days

18. Where was disease contracted if not at place of death? *93c*

Did an operation precede death? *no* Date of
Was there an autopsy? *no*
What test confirmed diagnosis? *clinical*

(Signed) *E. McCandless* M.D.
Aug. 20, 19 35 (Address) *Franklin Pa.*

* State the DISEASE CAUSING DEATH, or in deaths from VIOLENT CAUSES, state (1) MEANS AND NATURE OF INJURY, and (2) whether ACCIDENTAL, SUICIDAL, or HOMICIDAL. (See reverse side for additional space.)

19. PLACE OF BURIAL, CREMATION OR REMOVAL *Hickory Grove Cemetery*

DATE OF BURIAL *August 22* 19 35

20. UNDERTAKER *W. J. Barron*

ADDRESS *Franklin Pa.*

(OVER)

COMMONWEALTH OF PENNSYLVANIA
DEPARTMENT OF HEALTH
BUREAU OF VITAL STATISTICS

63054

Primary Dist. No. 61-04-21

File No. _______

CERTIFICATE OF DEATH

Registered No. 187

Exact Statement of OCCUPATION is very important. See Instructions on back of certificate. OF DEATH in plain terms, so that it may be properly classified.

1. PLACE OF DEATH:
(a) County...... Venango
(b) Township......
(c) Borough......
(d) City...... Franklin
(e) Name of hospital or institution...... 1115 Chestnut St.
(If not in hospital or inst. write street number or location)
(f) Length of stay: In hospital or inst...... (g) In this community 64Yrs.

2. USUAL RESIDENCE OF DECEASED:
(a) State Penna. (b) County Venango
(c) City or town Franklin
(If outside city or town limits, write RURAL)
(d) Street No. 1115 Chestnut St.
(If rural give location)
(e) If foreign born, how long in U. S. A.? ______ years.

3. (a) FULL NAME Mrs. Minnie Jane Oesau

3. (b) If U. S. Veteran, complete reverse side of certificate | 3 (c) Social Security No. X

5. Color or race W | 6. (a) Single, widowed, married, divorced W

4. Sex F

6. (b) Name of husband or wife John L. Oesau | 6 (c) Age of husband or wife if alive ______ years

7. Birth date of deceased Sept. 5, 1867
(Month) (Day) (Year)

8. AGE: Years 78 | Months 11 | Days 9 | If less than one day ___ hr. ___ min.

9. Birthplace Clinton Twp. Ven. Co., Pa.
(City, town, or county) (State or foreign country)

10. Usual occupation Housewife

11. Industry or business ______

MOTHER   FATHER

12. Name George McSparren

13. Birthplace Venango County, Pa.
(City, town, or county) (State or foreign country)

14. Maiden name Rachael Sutton

15. Birthplace Venango County, Pa.
(City, town, or county) (State or foreign country)

16. (a) Informant's own signature Dorene H. Oesau
(b) Address 1115 Chestnut St., Franklin

17. (a) Burial (b) Date thereof July 17, 1946
(Burial, cremation, or removal) (Month) (Day) (Year)
(c) Place Franklin County Venango State Pa.

18. (a) Signature of funeral director L L Burger
(b) Address 1315 Chestnut St Franklin Pa

19. (a) 7-16-46 (b) Bessie A. Brady
(Date received local registrar) (Registrar's signature)

MEDICAL CERTIFICATION

20. Date of death: Month July day 14
year 1946 hour 9 minute 45 A.M.

21. I hereby certify that I attended the deceased from
_6-42_, 19__, to _7-14_, 19__; that I last saw her alive on _7-14_, 19__; and that death occurred on the date and hour stated above.

Immediate cause of death Chronic Myocarditis

DURATION 5 yrs

Due to ______

Due to ______

Other conditions ______
(Include pregnancy within 3 months of death)

Major findings:
Of operations ______ 93-d

Of autopsy ______

PHYSICIAN — Underline the cause to which death should be charged statistically.

22. If death was due to external causes, fill in the following:
(a) (Probably) Accident, suicide, or homicide (specify) ______
(b) Date of occurrence ______
(c) Where did injury occur? ______
(City or town) (County) (State)
(d) Did injury occur in or about home, on farm, in industrial place, in public place? ______
(Specify type of place)
While at work? ______ (e) Means of injury ______

23. Signature ______ (M. D. or other)
Address ______ Date signed 7-15-46

CERTIFICATE OF DEATH

Form V. S. No. 5—100M 7-27-25

COMMONWEALTH OF PENNSYLVANI
DEPARTMENT OF HEALTH
BUREAU OF VITAL STATISTICS

92449

1. **PLACE OF DEATH**

County of _Venango_

Township of _Sugarcreek_

or Borough of _______

or City of _______

Registration District No. _881_

Primary Registration District No. _13376_

Registered No. _156_

File No. _______

[If death occurred in a Hospital or Institution give its NAME instead of street and number.] _Franklin Hospital_

2. **FULL NAME** _George M. S. Barron_

PERSONAL AND STATISTICAL PARTICULARS

3. SEX _M_

4. COLOR OR RACE _W_

5. SINGLE, MARRIED, WIDOWED OR DIVORCED (write the word) _Married_

5a. If married, widowed or divorced HUSBAND of (or) WIFE of _Rachel Sutton_

6. DATE OF BIRTH (month, day and year) _Oct. 19 1845_

7. AGE — Years _81_ Months _0_ Days _14_ — IF LESS than 1 day ___ hrs. or ___ min.

8. OCCUPATION OF DECEASED
(a) Trade, profession or particular kind of work _Retired_
(b) General nature of industry, business or establishment in which employed (or employer)
(c) Name of employer

9. BIRTHPLACE (City or town) (State or country) _Pa_

10. NAME OF FATHER _?_

11. BIRTHPLACE OF FATHER (City or town) (State or country) _?_

12. MAIDEN NAME OF MOTHER _?_

13. BIRTHPLACE OF MOTHER (City or town) (State or country) _?_

14. Informant _B. M. McBarron_
(Address) _Oil City, Pa._

15. Filed _Sept 4_, 19_26_ _Elizabeth H. Burchfield_, REGISTRAR.

11—3184

MEDICAL CERTIFICATE OF DEATH

16. DATE OF DEATH _Sept 3 1926_ (Month) (Day) (Year)

17. I HEREBY CERTIFY, That I attended deceased from _9/2/26_, 19__ to _9/3/26_, 19__ that I last saw him alive or _9/3/26_, 19__ and that death occurred, on the date stated above, at _12_ A. m.

The CAUSE OF DEATH* was as follows:

Heart Block

_24 a - 90_

(duration) ___ yrs. ___ mos. ___ ds.

CONTRIBUTORY (SECONDARY) _Intramural Hemorrhage_

(duration) ___ yrs. ___ mos. ___ ds.

18. Where was disease contracted if not at place of death? ___

Did an operation precede death? _No_ Date of ___

Was there an autopsy? _No_

What test confirmed diagnosis? _Physical Diagnosis_

(Signed) _Henry Huth_, M. D.

_9/9/26_ 19__ (Address) _Franklin Pa._

*State the DISEASE CAUSING DEATH, or in deaths from VIOLENT CAUSES, stat (1) MEANS AND NATURE OF INJURY, AND (2) whether ACCIDENTAL, SUICIDAL, o HOMICIDAL. (See reverse side for additional space.)

19. PLACE OF BURIAL, CREMATION OR REMOVAL _Hickory Grove Pa_

DATE OF BURIAL _Sept 6_ 19__

20. UNDERTAKER _J. J. Barron_

ADDRESS _Franklin Pa_

COMMONWEALTH OF PENNSYLVANIA
DEPARTMENT OF HEALTH
BUREAU OF VITAL STATISTICS

CERTIFICATE OF DEATH

HVS-20010—150M—10-42

Primary Dist. No. 62-06 83

File No. 82880

Registered No. 446

1. PLACE OF DEATH:
(a) County _Warren_
(b) Township _Conewango_
(c) Borough
(d) City
(e) Name of hospital or institution _Warren State Hospital_ (If not in hospital or inst. write street number or location)
(f) Length of stay: In hospital or inst. _4 yrs. 1 day_ (g) In this community

2. USUAL RESIDENCE OF DECEASED:
(a) State _Penna._ (b) County _Venango_
(c) City or town _Emlenton_ (If outside city or town limits, write RURAL)
(d) Street No. (If rural give location)
(e) If citizen of foreign country, name country

3. (a) FULL NAME _CHARLES H. McSPARREN_

3. (b) If U. S. Veteran, complete reverse side of certificate
3. (c) Social Security No.

4. Sex _Male_ | 5. Color or race _white_ | 6. (a) Single, widowed, married, divorced _single_
6. (b) Name of husband or wife
6. (c) Age of husband or wife if alive _____ years
7. Birth date of deceased _February 15, 1874_ (Month) (Day) (Year)

8. AGE: Years _70_ | Months _6_ | Days _29_ | If less than one day _____ hr. _____ min.

9. Birthplace _Penna._ (City, town, or county) (State or foreign country)
10. Usual occupation _none_
11. Industry or business _none_

FATHER
12. Name _George McSparren_
13. Birthplace _Penna._ (City, town, or county) (State or foreign country)

MOTHER
14. Maiden name _Rachel Sutton_
15. Birthplace _Penna._ (City, town, or county) (State or foreign country)

16. (a) Informant's own signature _W. Earl Biddle, M.D._
(b) Address _Warren State Hospital_
17. (a) _Burial_ (Burial, cremation, or removal) (b) Date thereof _9-17-44_ (Month) (Day) (Year)
(c) Place _Oil City_ County _Ven_ State _Pa_
18. (a) Signature of funeral director
(b) Address _Oil City, Pa_
19. (a) _Sept. 16-1944_ (Date received local registrar) (b) _Anna McKay_ (Registrar's signature)

MEDICAL CERTIFICATION
20. Date of death: Month _September_ day _14_ year _1944_ hour _5_ minute _00_ AM.
21. I hereby certify that I attended the deceased from _September 13_, 19_40_ to _September 14_, 19_44_ that I last saw him alive on _September 13_, 19_44_ and that death occurred on the date and hour stated above.
Immediate cause of death _Carcinoma of Prostate_ — DURATION _1 yr._
Due to
Due to
Other conditions _Psychosis due to Alcohol_ (Include pregnancy within 3 months of death) _4½ yrs._

PHYSICIAN
Major findings:
Of operations
Of autopsy

Underline the cause to which death should be charged statistically.

22. If death was due to external causes, fill in the following:
(a) (Probably) Accident, suicide, or homicide (specify)
(b) Date of occurrence
(c) Where did injury occur? (City or town) (County) (State)
(d) Did injury occur in or about home, on farm, in industrial place, in public place? (Specify type of place)
While at work? (e) Means of injury
23. Signature _W. Earl Biddle_ (M. D. or other)
Address _Warren State Hosp._ Date signed _9/14/44_

---

14.   Alfred Herstine Umstead, born March 25, 1847 in Pennsylvania; died September 10, 1922 in Oil City, Venango Co, PA. He was the son of 28. Jacob Hunsberger Umstead and 29. Barbara Johnston Herstine. He married 15. Ida Frances Manross Bell Bef. 1891.

15.   Ida Frances Manross Bell, born March 04, 1864 in Venango Co, Pennsylvania; she died on January 15, 1931 in Oil City, Venango Co, PA, and buried in Grove Hill Cemetery. She was the daughter of 30. John Bell and 31. Miss. Manross.

More About Alfred Herstine Umstead:
Burial: Grove Hill Cemetery, Oil City, Venango, PA
More About Ida Frances Manross Bell:

Burial: Grove Hill Cemetery, Oil City, Venango, PA

Children of Alfred Umstead and Ida Bell are:

7   i.   Annetta 'Nettie' Bell Umstead, born January 25, 1891 in Pearl, Cranberry Twp, Venango Co, PA>of Rosary, Cranberry Twp, Venango, PA; died January 06, 1953 in Franklin Hospital, Venango Co, PA; married David William Sutton McSparren January 17, 1906 in Franklin, Venango, PA.

         ii.   Henry Lafeyette Umstead, born 1894 in Venango Co, PA.

       iii.   William Bryon Umstead, born August 29, 1896 in Venango Co, PA; died July 25, 1964 at Sugarcreek Twp, Venango Co, PA.

       iv.   Amos S. Umstead, born December 27, 1897 in Venango Co, PA; died March 26, 1982 in Franklin, Venango, PA.

        v.   Cellestia E. Umstead, born 1899 in Venango Co, PA.

       vi.   Rolland M. Umstead, born 1901 in Venango Co, PA.

      vii.   Karl Apolis Umstead, born August 13, 1903 in Venango Co, PA; died October 1976 in Franklin, Venango, PA.

     viii.   David A. Umstead, born 1906 in Venango Co, PA.

Form V. S. No. 5—50M. 6-29-16.

CERTIFICATE OF DEATH

COMMONWEALTH OF PENNSYLVANIA
DEPARTMENT OF HEALTH
BUREAU OF VITAL STATISTICS.

1. PLACE OF DEATH.
County of *Venango*
Township of *Sandy Creek*   Registration District No. *881*
or Borough of   Primary Registration District No. *3374*
or City of   (No. _____ St., _____ Ward.)

File No. _____
Registered No. *146*

[If death occurred in a Hospital or Institution, give its NAME, instead of street and number.]

2. FULL NAME *Alfred H. Umstead*

PERSONAL AND STATISTICAL PARTICULARS

3. SEX *Male*
4. COLOR OR RACE *White*
5. SINGLE, MARRIED, WIDOWED OR DIVORCED *Married*
6. DATE OF BIRTH *March 25 1847* (Month) (Day) (Year)
7. AGE *75* yrs. *5* mo. *16* ds.   If LESS than 1 day how many ...... hrs. or ...... min.?
8. OCCUPATION (a) Trade, profession, or particular kind of work *Farmer* (b) General nature of industry, business, or establishment in which employed (or employer)
9. BIRTHPLACE (State or Country) *Pa*
10. NAME OF FATHER *Jacob Umstead*
11. BIRTHPLACE OF FATHER (State or Country) *Pa*
12. MAIDEN NAME OF MOTHER *Barbara Hurshire*
13. BIRTHPLACE OF MOTHER (State or Country) *Pa*

THE ABOVE IS TRUE TO THE BEST OF MY KNOWLEDGE.
(Informant) *A. L. Umstead Jr.*
(Address) *Emlenton, Pa*

Sept. 13, 191__   *Anna Boland*   Local Registrar

MEDICAL CERTIFICATE OF DEATH

16. DATE OF DEATH *Sept. 10 1922* (Month) (Day) (Year)

17. I HEREBY CERTIFY, That I attended deceased from *May 22 1922*, to *Sept 10 1922*, that I last saw him alive on *Sept 8 1922*, and that death occurred, on the date stated above, at *6:00 A.* M. The CAUSE OF DEATH* was as follows: *Cerebral Hemorrhage*

74 (Duration) _____ yrs. _____ mos. _____ ds.

Contributory (Secondary.)
(Duration) _____ yrs. _____ mos. _____ ds.

(Signed) *F. M. McClelland* M. D.
Sept. 10, 19 22 (Address) *Franklin, Pa*

*State the DISEASE CAUSING DEATH; or in deaths from VIOLENT CAUSES, state (1) MEANS OF INJURY; and (2) whether ACCIDENTAL, SUICIDAL, or HOMICIDAL.

18. LENGTH OF RESIDENCE (For Hospitals, Institutions, Transients or Recent Residents.)
At Place of death _____ yrs. _____ mos. _____ ds.   In the State _____ yrs. _____ mos. _____ ds.
Where was disease contracted, If not at place of death?
Former or usual residence

19. PLACE OF BURIAL OR REMOVAL *Oil City, Pa*   DATE OF BURIAL *Sept 12 1922*
20. UNDERTAKER *Boyd N. Parks*   ADDRESS *Franklin, Pa*

Form V. S. No. 5

CERTIFICATE OF DEATH

COMMONWEALTH OF PENNSYLVANIA
DEPARTMENT OF HEALTH
BUREAU OF VITAL STATISTICS

10347

1. **PLACE OF DEATH**

County of _Venango_

Township of ....

or

Borough of ....

or

City of _Oil City Pa. / Hospital_

Registration District No. ....

Primary Registration District No. _61-05-01_

File No. ....

Registered No. _12_

[If death occurred in a Hospital or Institution give its NAME instead of street and number.]

2. FULL NAME _Mrs. Ida Francis Umstead_

(a) Residence. No. _2 Haliday St_ St., _3_ Ward.

(Usual place of abode)

Length of residence in city or town where death occurred ___ yrs. ___ mos. ___ ds. How long in U. S., if of foreign birth? ___ yrs. ___ mos. ___ ds.

(If nonresident give city or town and State)

PERSONAL AND STATISTICAL PARTICULARS

3. SEX _F_

4. COLOR OR RACE _W_

5. SINGLE, MARRIED, WIDOWED OR DIVORCED (*write the word*) _Widowed_

5a. If married, widowed, or divorced HUSBAND of (or) WIFE of _Carl Umstead_

6. DATE OF BIRTH (month, day, and year) _March 4 1864_

7. AGE — Years _67_ — Months _10_ — Days _9_ — IF LESS than 1 day ... hrs. or ... min.

8. OCCUPATION OF DECEASED

(a) Trade, profession, or particular kind of work _Retired_

(b) General nature of industry, business or establishment in which employed (or employer) ....

(c) Name of employer ....

9. BIRTHPLACE (city or town) _Penna_
(State or Country)

10. NAME OF FATHER _John Bell_

11. BIRTHPLACE OF FATHER (city or town) _Penna_
(State or Country)

12. MAIDEN NAME OF MOTHER _Dont Know_

13. BIRTHPLACE OF MOTHER (city or town) _"_
(State or Country)

14. Informant _T. G. Umstead_
(Address) _No 2 Haliday St Oil City Pa_

15. Filed _Jan 19_ 19_31_ _William J. Lewis_

REGISTRAR

MEDICAL CERTIFICATE OF DEATH

16. DATE OF DEATH _Jan_ (Month) _15_ (Day) _1931_ (Year)

17. I HEREBY CERTIFY, That I attended deceased from _Jan 15_ 19_31_ to _Jan 16_ 19_31_, that I last saw her alive on _Jan 16_ 19_31_, and that death occurred, on the date stated above, at _8.20 P._ m.

The CAUSE OF DEATH* was as follows:

Croupous Pneumonia

Tota

..................(duration) ___ yrs. ___ mos. _4_ days

CONTRIBUTORY ....
(Secondary)

..................(duration) ___ yrs. ___ Mos. ___ days

18. Where was disease contracted if not at place of death? ....

Did an operation precede death? _No_ Date of

Was there an autopsy? _No_

What test confirmed diagnosis? ....

(Signed) _K. A. Thomas_ M.D.

Jan 17 19_31_ (Address) _Oil City Pa_

*State the DISEASE CAUSING DEATH, or in deaths from VIOLENT CAUSES, state (1 MEANS AND NATURE OF INJURY, and (2) whether ACCIDENTAL, SUICIDAL, or HOMICIDAL. (See reverse side for additional space.)

19. PLACE OF BURIAL, CREMATION OR REMOVAL

Grove Hill Cemetry

20. UNDERTAKER _F. N. Osander_

DATE OF BURIAL

Jan 19 19_31_

ADDRESS _Oil City Pa_

(OVER)

Generation No. 5

(Great Great Grandparents)

Found: 16 of 16

16. *Matthias Syrus Culver*, born April 01, 1853 in Washington Twp, Erie Co, PA > Crawford Co, PA; died January 01, 1898 in Blooming Valley, Crawford Co, Pennsylvania >Blooming Valley Cemetery. He was the son of 32. Joseph H. Culver and 33. Sarah Cole. He married 17. Marilla "Rillie" E. Davison June 21, 1874 in Erie, Erie Co, PA.

17. *Marilla "Rillie" E. Davison*, born January 21, 1857 in PA >; died May 28, 1883 in Blooming Valley, Crawford Co, PA> Blooming Valley Cemetery. She was the daughter of 34. Sellick Davison and 35. Mary A. Perham.

Notes for Matthias Lyrus Culver:
1880 Census, Mathias, wife Murilla and children living in Richmond, Crawford Co, PA

Children of Matthias Culver and Marilla Davison are:

  i. Cecil Carl Culver, born March 11, 1876 in Girard, Erie County, Pennsylvania >Rouseville, PA; died May 09, 1952 in Wyandotte, Ottawa Co, Oklahoma >Wyandotte Indian Cemetery; married Elizabeth Patterson August 20, 1900 in Oil City, PA; born 1877 in County Armagh, Ireland>came to America at age 16; died 1970 in Wyandotte, Ottawa Co, Oklahoma >Wyandotte Indian Cemetery.
   Notes for Cecil Carl Culver:
   Find A Grave Memorial# 143411962
   1880 living in Richmond Twp, Crawford Co, PA
   1900 living in Shippen, Cameron, PA
   1910 living in Oil City, Venango Co, Pennsylvania
   1920 living in Nowata, Nowata Co, Oklahoma
   1930 living in Strike Axe Twp, Osage County, Oklahoma
   Notes for Elizabeth Patterson:
   Find A Grave Memorial# 143412135

8 ii. Carson Earl Culver, born October 21, 1877 in Edinboro, Erie Co, Pennsylvania >of Franklin, Erie Co, PA in 1910; died February 01, 1948 in Capitol Heights, Prince George's County, Maryland; married Mabel Mae Holt July 26, 1898 in Washington Twp, Erie County, Pennsylvania.

  iii. Cherie "Ree" H. Culver, born October 26, 1879 in Pennsylvania; died May 26, 1946 in Erie, Erie Co, PA > Erie Cemetery; married Claud N. Ore; born 1872; died 1929 in Erie, Erie Co, PA > Erie Cemetery.

REGISTRATION CARD

SERIAL NUMBER 1238 ORDER NUMBER A-1975

1. Cecil Carl Culver
2. Box 1016, Nowata, Nowata Co, Okla
3. Age in Years 42 4. Date of Birth March 11th, 1876

RACE

White ✓ | Negro | Oriental | Indian Citizen | Noncitizen

U. S. CITIZEN | ALIEN

Native Born ✓ | Naturalized | Citizen by Father's Naturalization Before Registrant's Majority | Declarant | Non-declarant

16. PRESENT OCCUPATION Farming
17. EMPLOYER'S NAME Farm for myself
18. PLACE OF EMPLOYMENT OR BUSINESS: Nowata Co, Okla

19. NEAREST RELATIVE Name Elizabeth Patterson Culver
Address Box 1016 Nowata, Nowata Co, Okla

I AFFIRM THAT I HAVE VERIFIED ABOVE ANSWERS AND THAT THEY ARE TRUE.
Cecil Carl Culver

REGISTRAR'S REPORT 35-2-14-C

DESCRIPTION OF REGISTRANT

HEIGHT: Tall ✓ | Medium | Short
BUILD: Slender | Medium ✓ | Stout
COLOR OF EYES Blue COLOR OF HAIR Brown

Has person lost arm, leg, hand, eye, or is he obviously physically disqualified? (Specify) No

I certify that my answers are true; that the person registered has read or has had read to him his own answers, that I have witnessed his signature or mark, and that all of his answers of which I have knowledge are true, except as follows:

Allern Picians

Date of Registration Sepa 12 - 1918

Local Board
Nowata County, Oklahoma,
(NAME OF LOCAL BOARD)

The stamp of the Local Board having jurisdiction of the area in which the registrant has his permanent home shall be placed in this box.

HVS-20009

COMMONWEALTH OF PENNSYLVANIA
DEPARTMENT OF HEALTH
BUREAU OF VITAL STATISTICS

Primary Dist. No. 25-04-01

CERTIFICATE OF DEATH

File No. 42395 Registered No. 647 600

1. PLACE OF DEATH:
(a) County Erie
(b) City or borough or township Erie
(c) Name of hospital or institution 2609 East Avenue
(If not in hospital or institution write street number or location)
(d) Length of stay: In hospital or institution
In this community years, months or days (Specify whether)

2. USUAL RESIDENCE OF DECEASED:
(a) State Pa. (b) County Erie
(c) City or town Erie (If outside city or town limits, write RURAL)
(d) Street No. 2609 East Avenue (If rural give location)
(e) If foreign born, how long in U. S. A.? ___ years.

3. (a) FULL NAME Ree H. Culver Ore
3. (b) If U. S. Veteran, complete reverse side of certificate
3. (c) Social Security No.
4. Sex F 5. Color or race W 6. (a) Single, widowed, married, divorced widowed
6. (b) Name of husband or wife Claud N. Ore
6. (c) Age of husband or wife if alive ___ years
7. Birth date of deceased Oct. 26, 1879 (Month) (Day) (Year)
8. AGE: Years 66 | Months 7 | Days 0 | If less than one day ___ hr. ___ min.
9. Birthplace Erie County, Pa. (City, town, or county) (State or foreign country)
10. Usual occupation At home
11. Industry or business
FATHER: 12. Name Mathias Culver
13. Birthplace Not known (City, town, or county) (State or foreign country)
MOTHER: 14. Maiden name Narilla --------
15. Birthplace Not known (City, town, or county) (State or foreign country)
16. (a) Informant's own signature Elizabeth Money
(b) Address 2609 East Ave.
17. (a) Burial (b) Date thereof 5/29/46 (Month) (Day) (Year)
(Burial, cremation, or removal)
Erie County
(c) Place: burial or cremation Erie Cemetery
18. (a) Signature of funeral director Chester A. Schaal
(b) Address 550 West 9th St. Erie Pa.
19. (a) 5-28-46 (Date received local registrar)
(b) Joseph Hurley (Registrar's signature)

MEDICAL CERTIFICATION
20. Date of death: Month May day 26th
year 1946 hour 4: minute 15 AM
21. I hereby certify that I attended the deceased from 4-10-45, 19__, to 5-26-46, 19__;
that I last saw her alive on 5-25-46, 19__;
and that death occurred on the date and hour stated above.
Immediate cause of death
Cardiac insufficiency DURATION 2 yrs
Due to Chronic hypertensive cardiovascular renal disease. 5 yrs
Due to
Other conditions (Include pregnancy within 3 months of death)
Major findings:
Of operations n/a
Of autopsy 95 c
PHYSICIAN Underline the cause to which death should be charged statistically.

22. If death was due to external causes, fill in the following:
(a) (Probably) Accident, suicide, or homicide (specify)
(b) Date of occurrence
(c) Where did injury occur? (City or town) (County) (State)
(d) Did injury occur in or about home, on farm, in industrial place, in public place? (Specify type of place)
While at work? (e) Means of injury
23. Signature B.E. Becker MD (M. D. or other)
Address 2527 Reed st., Erie, Pa. Date signed 5-27-46

further development, he and his family occupy a beautiful home in the city of Bartlesville, where they are surrounded by all of the comforts and many of the luxuries of life.

C. C. CULVER.

One of the prominent residents of Nowata is C. C. Culver, proprietor of the Westview Jersey Farm and a breeder of registered stock. He was born at Girard, Erie county, Pennsylvania, on the 11th of March, 1876, and received his education in Crawford county, putting his textbooks aside after completing a business course. From that time until 1907 he engaged in the oil business, achieving substantial success, but in 1907 determined to dispose of his interests and come west. He had had some dairying experience in his early youth, his father, Si Culver, having been engaged in the dairy business for many years in association with William Fairweather, an Ayrshire breeder in Pennsylvania. Upon first coming to Nowata, however, Mr. Culver again engaged in the oil business but in 1913 made his initial step into the dairy business here. He started with grade Jerseys and now has fifteen head of registered Jersey cows and forty-five head of grade Jerseys. He has a Jersey bull, Majesty's Financial Gyp, No. 177,140, who is a grandson of Financial Countess's Lad, the sire of Financial Sensation, who sold for sixty thousand dollars, whose service cost five hundred dollars and whose dame gave over three hundred and forty pounds of butter fat per year. Majesty's Financial Gyp is a son of Noble's Western Count, No. 151,953, by Noble Western King, herd bull of the Elmdorf Farm at Lexington, Kentucky. He then goes to Raleigh's Fairy Boy, sire of forty registered merit daughters. Mr. Culver owns the half sister of Financial Sensation, her name being Countess Lad's Buttercup, No. 350,263, and he also owns a great-granddaughter of Countess Lad's, called Countess Lad's Peggy. Eminence Majesty, No. 146,279, a half brother of Majesty's Little Princess, the four-year-old champion of Oklahoma, belongs to Mr. Culver, as does Oxford Double You'll Do, who runs in the fourth cross to Gamboyes' Knight, an undefeated bull, and on the mother's side she goes to Gamboyes' Knight again in the fourth cross. Her maternal grandmother is Clover

Queeney, No. 232,261, who is a granddaughter of Stoke Pogis of Prospect, No. 64,807, sire of sixty-seven tested daughters, including Olga's Fourth Pride, who made one thousand and two pounds and six ounces of butter in one year. Her half sister, Adelaide of Blochland, made nine hundred and ninety-nine pounds and eight and nine-tenths ounces of butter in one year. Mr. Culver has shown her in all of the state fairs and she has never been defeated in the junior class. Mr. Culver is milking twenty-seven cows a day and sells about two hundred quarts of bottled milk in Nowata. He employs three men and uses three hundred acres of land as pasturage for his cattle. He owns the stock, but his partner, W. R. Dawson, owns the buildings on the land. It is the ambition of Mr. Culver to own a herd as good as the herd which was formerly on this same dairy farm and which is now owned by J. E. Jones of Liberty, Missouri, who built the equipment for this dairy farm, known as the Westview Jersey Farm, and is one of the big breeders of fine stock in this part of the United States.

In 1899 occurred the marriage of Mr. Culver to Miss Elizabeth Patterson, a native of County Armagh, Ireland, who came to this country and located in Pennsylvania when she was but sixteen years of age. To the union of Mr. and Mrs. Culver nine children have been born. Those living are: Ella, Dorothy, William, Leonard and Bruce. Those who have passed away are: Garnett, Cecil, and Jack and Dick, twins.

Mr. Culver is thoroughly familiar with every phase of the dairy and cattle breeding business and he has won for himself an enviable place among the cattlemen of Oklahoma. He is never too busy to give his aid in the furtherance of any movement for the development and improvement of the community and is conceded to be one of the representative citizens of Nowata.

18. Eli Mark Holt, born April 24, 1849 in Ohio > Washington Twp, Erie Co, PA in 1900; died November 18, 1932 in Edinboro, Erie Co, Pennsylvania burial in Edinboro Cemetery. He was the son of 36. Elijah Holt and 37. Laura A. Conant. He married 19. Isabelle H. 'Belle' Wicks Bef. 1879.

19. Isabelle H. 'Belle' Wicks, born April 18, 1847 in McLane, Erie Co, Pennsylvania; died August 06, 1934 in Edinboro, Erie Co, Pennsylvania burial in Edinboro Cemetery. She was the daughter of 38. Jeremiah Smith Wicks and 39. Harriet Conant.

Notes for Eli Mark Holt:
Find A Grave Memorial# 157123977
Notes for Isabelle H. 'Belle' Wicks:
Find A Grave Memorial# 157124038

Children of Eli Holt and Isabelle Wicks are:
       i.   Oracut Holt, born 1867 in Pennsylvania.
      ii.   Nora Holt, born 1871 in Michigan; died 1946 in Edinboro, Erie Co, Pennsylvania burial in Edinboro Cemetery; married Harned.
9   iii.   Mabel Mae Holt, born May 30, 1879 in Leavitt, Oceana Co, Michigan >of Oakland Twp, Venango Co, PA in 1900; died January 15, 1942; married Carson Earl Culver July 26, 1898 in Washington Twp, Erie County, Pennsylvania.
      iv.   Guy Holt, born 1880 in Pennsylvania.
      v.   Robert R. Holt, born 1882 in Pennsylvania.

20. Levi DeRemer, born December 24, 1840 in New York; he relocated to Meadville, Crawford Co, Pennsylvania. Levi died on November 7, 1880 in Crawford County, PA and is buried in the Wayland Cemetery. He was the son of 40. Joseph DeRemer and 41. Rachel Jones. Levi married 21. Irena Heath bef 1867.

21. Irene Heath, born August 3, 1843 in Randolph Twp, Crawford Co, PA. She died on May 4, 1921 in Troy Twp, Crawford Co, Pennsylvania and is buried at Wayland Cemetery. She was the daughter of 42. Hazen H. Heath and 43. Mary 'Polly' Cain or Kane. Irene married a 2nd time to George Coy.

Burial data for Levi DeRemer
Find A Grave Memorial# 125562799
Burial data for Irene Coy DeRemer:
Find A Grave Memorial# 177271970

Children of Levi DeRemer and Irene Heath:
      i.   William L. DeRemer born 1867
10   ii.   George William DeRemer born May 1, 1869

iii.   Fred Joseph DeRemer born December 25, 1877

rm V. S. No. 5—100M-4-23-19.

PLACE OF DEATH

County of *Crawford*

Township of *Troy*

or

Borough of

or

City of (No.   St.   Ward.)

[If death occurred in a Hospital or Institution, give its NAME instead of street and number.]

COMMONWEALTH OF PENNSYLVANIA
DEPARTMENT OF HEALTH
BUREAU OF VITAL STATISTICS.

CERTIFICATE OF DEATH

Registration District No. *436*

Primary Registration District No. *2055*

File No. *51375*

Registered No. *53*

2. FULL NAME *Irene Coy*

PERSONAL AND STATISTICAL PARTICULARS	MEDICAL CERTIFICATE OF DEATH

3. SEX *F* | 4. COLOR OR RACE *W* | 5. SINGLE, MARRIED, WIDOWED OR DIVORCED (*Write the word.*) *Widow*

16. DATE OF DEATH *May 4 1921* (Month) (Day) (Year)

6. DATE OF BIRTH *Aug. 3 1843* (Month) (Day) (Year)

17. I HEREBY CERTIFY, That I attended deceased from *April 20* 1921, to *May 4*, 1921, that I last saw her alive on *April 28* 1921, and that death occurred, on the date stated above, at *1 P.* M. The CAUSE OF DEATH* was as follows:

7. AGE yrs. *77* mos. *9* ds. *1* | If LESS than 1 day how many......hrs. or ......min ?

Acute indigestion

(Duration) *1/2* yrs.   mos. *14* ds.

8. OCCUPATION — Trade, profession, or, particular kind of work — General nature of industry, business, or establishment in which employed (or employer)

Contributory (Secondary.)

(Duration)   yrs.   mos.   ds.

9. BIRTHPLACE. (State or Country) *Penna*

10. NAME OF FATHER *Henry Heath*

(Signed) *W. J. Richey* M. D.

11. BIRTHPLACE OF FATHER (State or Country) *York State, N.Y.*

May 5 1921 (Address) *Diamond, Pa.*

12. MAIDEN NAME OF MOTHER *Mary Cain*

*State the DISEASE CAUSING DEATH; or in deaths from VIOLENT CAUSES, state (1) MEANS OF INJURY; and (2) whether ACCIDENTAL, SUICIDAL, or HOMICIDAL.

13. BIRTHPLACE OF MOTHER (State or Country) *York State, N.Y.*

18. LENGTH OF RESIDENCE (For Hospitals, Institutions, Transients or Recent Residents). At place of death.....yrs.....mos.....ds. In the State.....yrs.....mos.....ds. Where was disease contracted, if not at place of death ? Former or usual residence

THE ABOVE IS TRUE TO THE BEST OF MY KNOWLEDGE:

(Informant) *Dave DeRemer*

(Address) *Townville, Pa*

19. PLACE OF BURIAL OR REMOVAL *Wayland Cemetery* | DATE OF BURIAL *May 7 1921*

Filed *5/6* 1921 *Rob't Akers* Local Registrar

20. UNDERTAKER *Willie L. Arnold* | ADDRESS *Townville*

---

22. *Jacob C. Clark*, born in March 15, 1854-62 in Crawford Co, Pennsylvania, he died October 16, 1924 at Corry, Erie Co, PA and is buried at a Townville, PA Cemetery. He was the son of 44. John Clark and 45. Dorcas Hoffman. He married 23. Jenny Mae Coy in 1877 in Crawford Co, Pennsylvania. He married a 2nd time on April 28, 1922, Mrs. Alice Wallace Stearns at Tionesta, Forest Co, PA.

23. *Jenny Mae Coy*, born April 24, 1857 in Pennsylvania; she died July 14, 1920 at Townville, Crawford Co, Pennsylvania and is buried at a Townville, PA Cemetery. She was the daughter of 46. George Coy and 47. Mary Jane Knapp.

Notes on Jacob & Jenny Clark:
1880 Census, family living in Blooming Valley Twp, Crawford Co, PA; one daughter, Minnie Clark age 3.
1900 Census, family living in Troy Twp, Crawford Co, PA, 7 children listed.
1920 Census, they were living in Union City, Erie Co, PA; in household of their daughter, Fern Toner and her husband, Patsy and their children.

Children of Jacob Clark and Jenny Coy are:

11	i.	Minnie Mae Clark, born September 29, 1877 in Blooming Valley, Crawford Co, PA; died May 05, 1917 in Meadville, Crawford Co, Pennsylvania; married George William DeRemer March 06, 1893 in Pennsylvania.
	ii.	George Clark, born 1880 in Crawford Co, PA.
	iii.	Mary Clark, born 1881 in Crawford Co, PA.
	iv.	Frank Clark, born 1883 in Crawford Co, PA.
	v.	Pearl A. Clark, born 1887 in Crawford Co, PA.
	vi.	Dora Clark, born 1890 in Crawford Co, PA.
	vii.	Fern E. Clark, born 1891 in Crawford Co, PA. She married Patsy Toner b. 1875.
	viii.	James Clark, born 1893 in Crawford Co, PA.
	ix.	Julia A. Clark, born 1900 in Crawford Co, PA.

Form V. S. No. 5—50M-1-11-23

CERTIFICATE OF DEATH

COMMONWEALTH OF PENNSYLVANIA
DEPARTMENT OF HEALTH
BUREAU OF VITAL STATISTICS

1. **PLACE OF DEATH**

County of Erie — Registration District No. 501 — 462 — File No. 94593

Township of ______ or Borough of ______ — Primary Registration District No. 35 — Registered No. 102

City of Corry, Pa. — (No. ______ Corry Hospital St., 3. Ward) [If death occurred in a Hospital or Institution give its NAME instead of street and number.]

2. **FULL NAME** Jacob C. Clark.

PERSONAL AND STATISTICAL PARTICULARS

3. SEX: Male

4. COLOR OR RACE: White

5. SINGLE, MARRIED, WIDOWED OR DIVORCED (write the word): Married

5a. If married, widowed, or divorced HUSBAND of (or) WIFE of: Miss Alice Stearns

6. DATE OF BIRTH (month, day, and year): May 15th 1852

7. AGE: Years 72 | Months 5 | Days 1. | IF LESS than 1 day, ___hrs. or ___min.

8. OCCUPATION OF DECEASED
(a) Trade, profession, or particular kind of work: Farmer
(b) General nature of industry, business, or establishment in which employed (or employer):
(c) Name of employer:

9. BIRTHPLACE (city or town) (State or country): Penna.

10. NAME OF FATHER: John Clark

11. BIRTHPLACE OF FATHER (city or town) (State or country): U.S.

12. MAIDEN NAME OF MOTHER: Do Not Know

13. BIRTHPLACE OF MOTHER (city or town) (State or country): Do Not Know

14. Informant: James Clark
(Address) Corry Pa. 152 N. Smyth

15. Filed Oct. 17, 1924 ______ Registrar
11—3184

MEDICAL CERTIFICATE OF DEATH

16. DATE OF DEATH: Oct. (Month) 16. (Day) 1924 (Year)

17. I HEREBY CERTIFY, That I attended deceased from, Oct. 12, 1924, to Oct. 16, 1924 that I last saw him alive on Oct. 16, 1924 and that death occurred, on the date stated above, at 9.00 P. m.
The CAUSE OF DEATH* was as follows:
Nephritis
129-90 about 2 (duration) yrs. mos. ds.

CONTRIBUTORY (SECONDARY) Myocarditis Indefinite (duration) yrs. mos. ds.

18. Where was disease contracted if not at place of death? Don't know
Did an operation precede death? No Date of —
Was there an autopsy? No
What test confirmed diagnosis? Clinical
(Signed) G. D. Bennett M. D.
19 (Address) Corry Pa

*State the DISEASE CAUSING DEATH, or in deaths from VIOLENT CAUSES, state (1) MEANS and NATURE OF INJURY, and (2) whether ACCIDENTAL, SUICIDAL, or HOMICIDAL. (See reverse side for additional space.)

19. PLACE OF BURIAL, CREMATION OR REMOVAL: Burial At Townville, Penna.
DATE OF BURIAL: Oct. 18, 1924

20. UNDERTAKER: Alexander & Company
ADDRESS: Corry, Penna.

Form V. S. No. 5—50M-1-8-14.

CERTIFICATE OF DEATH

COMMONWEALTH OF PENNSYLVANIA.
DEPARTMENT OF HEALTH
BUREAU OF VITAL STATISTICS.
462

1. PLACE OF DEATH

County of Crawford — Registration District No. 436 — File No. 89953

Township of Troy or Borough of ______ — Primary Registration District No. 2533 — Registered No. 93

City of Townville — (No. ______ , St., ______ Ward.) [If death occurred in a Hospital or Institution, give its NAME instead of street and number.]

2. FULL NAME Mrs Jennie May Clark

PERSONAL AND STATISTICAL PARTICULARS

3. SEX: Female

4. COLOR OR RACE: White

5. SINGLE, MARRIED, WIDOWED OR DIVORCED (Write the word.): Married

6. DATE OF BIRTH: April 24 1862 (Month) (Day) (Year)

7. AGE: yrs 58 mos 2 ds 8 | If LESS than 1 day how many ...... hrs. or ...... min. ?

8. OCCUPATION
(a) Trade, profession, or particular kind of work: House Wife
(b) General nature of industry, business, or establishment in which employed (or employer):

9. BIRTHPLACE (State or Country): Penn.

10. NAME OF FATHER: George Coy

11. BIRTHPLACE OF FATHER (State or Country): Penn.

12. MAIDEN NAME OF MOTHER: Mary Knapp

13. BIRTHPLACE OF MOTHER (State or Country): Penn

14. THE ABOVE IS TRUE TO THE BEST OF MY KNOWLEDGE.
(Informant) Dewey Lingo
(Address) Townville Pa

15. Filed 7/19/ 1920 Robt A. Kerr
Local Registrar

MEDICAL CERTIFICATE OF DEATH

16. DATE OF DEATH: July 14 1920 (Month) (Day) (Year)

17. I HEREBY CERTIFY, That I attended deceased from Jan. 17, 1917, to Date 191__ that I last saw her alive on June 14 1920 and that death occurred, on the date stated above, at 1:30 P. M.
The CAUSE OF DEATH* was as follows:
Acute Oedema of the Lungs
81-94 (Duration) X yrs. X mos. ½ ds.

Contributory (Secondary) Arterio-Sclerosis General (Duration) 3 yrs. 6 mos. X ds.

(Signed) Wm. H. Gray M. D.
July 15 1920 (Address) Townville Pa.

*State the DISEASE CAUSING DEATH; or in deaths from VIOLENT CAUSES, state (1) MEANS OF INJURY; and (2) whether ACCIDENTAL, SUICIDAL, or HOMICIDAL.

18. LENGTH OF RESIDENCE (For Hospitals, Institutions, Transients or Recent Residents).
At Place of death ...yrs. ...mos. ...ds. In the State ...yrs. ...mos. ...ds.
Where was disease contracted, If not at place of death?
Former or usual residence

19. PLACE OF BURIAL OR REMOVAL: Townville, Pa
DATE OF BURIAL: July 15 1920

20. UNDERTAKER: Van Tassel
ADDRESS: Union City, Pa.

24. *Robert McSparren*, born c.1815 in Pennsylvania. In 1840 this family was living in Irvin Twp, Venango Co, PA; he died ____________ at ______________.

25. *Mrs. McSparren*, born c.1815 in Pennsylvania.

They were the parents of:
12.   i.   George W. McSparren - he married Rachel Sutton.

26. *Reuben Sutton*, born 1788 in Maryland >1860 lives in Irwin, Venango Co, PA; died 1865. He married 27. Elizabeth 'Eliza' Ann Alcorn Bef. 1832 in Venango Co, PA.

27. *Elizabeth 'Eliza' Ann Alcorn*, born 1810 in Maryland >1860 lives in Irwin, Venango Co, PA; died 1872.

Children of Reuben Sutton and Elizabeth Alcorn are:
       i.   Adam C. Dr. Sutton, born January 02, 1832 in Irwin, Venango Co, PA; died January 08, 1912 in Franklin, Venango Co, PA; married Esther; born Abt. 1833 in Pennsylvania.
           Notes for Adam C. Dr. Sutton:
           Find A Grave Memorial# 140605189
      ii.   Hiram Smith Sutton, born March 31, 1836 in Irwin, Venango Co, PA; died August 05, 1907 in Sandy Creek, Venango Co, PA; married Emily DeWoody; born 1846; died 1929.
           Notes for Hiram Smith Sutton:
           Find A Grave Memorial# 153938721
     iii.   John G. Sutton, born 1838 in Irwin, Venango Co, PA; died Bef. 1926 in Rocky Grove, Sugar Creek, Venango Co, PA; married Angeline L. Whaley; born March 14, 1843 in Scrubgrass, PA; died November 29, 1926 in Rocky Grove, Sugar Creek, Venango Co, PA.
     iv.   Rebecca Ann Sutton, born 1840 in Irwin, Venango Co, PA.
13   v.   Rachel Carroll Sutton, born June 23, 1844 in Irwin, Venango Co, PA; died December 02, 1929 in Venango Co, PA > Hickory Grove Cemetery; married George W. McSparren Bef. 1867 in Pennsylvania.
     vi.   William E. Sutton, born 1846 in Irwin, Venango Co, PA.
    vii.   Alvin Sutton, born 1849 in Irwin, Venango Co, PA.

28. *Jacob Hunsberger Umstead*, born October 18, 1809 in Illinois City, PA; died January 24, 1894 in Oil City, Venango Co, PA >Grove Hill Cemetery. He was the son of 56. Joel Tyson Umstead and 57. Anna Tyson Hunsberger. He married 29. Barbara Johnston Herstine Abt. 1846 in Pennsylvania.

29. *Barbara Johnston Herstine*, born October 13, 1828 in Pennsylvania; died February 06, 1913 in Oil City, Venango Co, PA >Grove Hill Cemetery.

Children of Jacob Umstead and Barbara Herstine are:

14   i.   Alfred Herstine Umstead, born March 25, 1847 in Pennsylvania; died September 10, 1922 in Oil City, Venango Co, PA; married (1) Jannett Crawford Abt. 1860; married (2) Ida Frances Manross Bell Bef. 1891.

     ii.   Elizabeth Herstine Umstead, born Abt. 1849 in Pennsylvania.

     iii.   Nancy Herstine Umstead, born Abt. 1851 in Pennsylvania.

     iv.   Sarah Herstine Umstead, born Abt. 1852 in Pennsylvania.

30. *John Bell*, born c.1840 at __________; he died ______ at _________ and is buried at ___________ Cemetery. John was the son of 60. _________ Bell and 61. ___________. He married 31. ________ Manross.

31. _______ *Manross*, born Bet. 1840 - 1850 in Venango Co, PA. She was the daughter of 62. William Harrison Manross and 63. Margaret Callen.

Child of John Bell and Miss Manross is:

15   i.   Ida Frances Manross Bell, born March 04, 1864 in Pennsylvania; died January 15, 1931 in Oil City, Venango Co, PA >Grove Hill Cemetery; married Alfred Herstine Umstead Bef. 1891.

Form V. S. No. 5—50M. 6-22-11.

CERTIFICATE OF DEATH.

COMMONWEALTH OF PENNSYLVANIA
DEPARTMENT OF HEALTH
BUREAU OF VITAL STATISTICS

1. PLACE OF DEATH.
County of *Venango*
Township of
or Borough of
or City of *Franklin*

Registration District No. *881*
Primary Registration District No. *37—6*
File No. *2357*
Registered No. *5*
No. *Chestnut* St.

[If death occurred in a Hospital or Institution, give its NAME instead of street and number.]

2. FULL NAME *Adam. C Sutton*

PERSONAL AND STATISTICAL PARTICULARS | MEDICAL CERTIFICATE OF DEATH

3. SEX *Male*
4. COLOR OR RACE *White*
5. SINGLE, MARRIED, WIDOWED OR DIVORCED (Write the word.) *Widowed*
6. DATE OF BIRTH *Jan 2 1832* (Month) (Day) (Year)
7. AGE *80* yrs. — mos. *5* ds. If LESS than 1 day how many......hrs. or ......min.?
8. OCCUPATION
(a) Trade, profession, or particular kind of work
(b) General nature of industry business, or establishment in which employed (or employer) *Physician*
9. BIRTHPLACE (State or Country) *Mercer Co Pa*
10. NAME OF FATHER *Sutton.*
11. BIRTHPLACE OF FATHER (State or Country) *Penna*
12. MAIDEN NAME OF MOTHER *Elizabeth Alcorn*
13. BIRTHPLACE OF MOTHER (State or Country) *Penna*
14. THE ABOVE IS TRUE TO THE BEST OF MY KNOWLEDGE.
(Informant) *Mrs E E Hamer*
(Address) *Franklin Pa*
15. Filed *Jan 9 1912* *E Baland* Local Registrar

16. DATE OF DEATH *Jan 8 1912* (Month) (Day) (Year)
17. I HEREBY CERTIFY, That I attended deceased from ......191... to ......191...
that I last saw h...... alive on ......191...
and that death occurred, or the date stated above, at *8.30 A* M.
The CAUSE OF DEATH was as follows: *Exposure*
(Duration) ......yrs. ......mos. ......ds.
Contributory (Secondary)
(Duration) ......yrs. ......mos. ......ds.
(Signed) *Albert McEvoy Conner* M. D.
Jan. 9. 1912 (Address) *Oil City Pa*

*State the DISEASE CAUSING DEATH; or in deaths from VIOLENT CAUSES, state (1) MEANS OF INJURY; and (2) whether ACCIDENTAL, SUICIDAL, or HOMICIDAL.

18. LENGTH OF RESIDENCE (For Hospitals, Institutions, Transients or Recent Residents).
At place of death......yrs......mos......ds. In the State......yrs......mos......ds
Where was disease contracted, if not at place of death?
Former or usual residence

19. PLACE OF BURIAL OR REMOVAL *Franklin Cemetery*
DATE OF BURIAL *Jan 9 1912*
20. UNDERTAKER *H J Byrer* ADDRESS *Franklin. Pa.*

Generation No. 6

(Great Great Great Grandparents)
Found: 20 of 32

32. *Joseph H. Culver*, born October 20, 1822 in Wilkes Farm, Crawford Co, PA; died September 16, 1893 in Townville, Crawford Co, PA >Kingsley Cemetery. He was the son of 64. Joseph Sr. Culver and 65. Pheba Johnston. He married 33. Sarah Cole Bef. 1842 in Crawford Co, PA.

33. *Sarah Cole*, born 1822 in New York > Crawford Co, PA; died September 1880 in Townville, Crawford Co, PA >Kingsley Cemetery. She was the daughter of 66. Jacobus 'Jacob' Cole and 67. Rachel.

Notes for Joseph H. Culver:

1850, Joseph & Sarah with 4 kids living at Woodcock twp, Crawford Co, PA.
1860, Joseph & Sarah with 5 children living in Richmond Twp, Crawford Co, PA. Next 3 houses down live the Cole families. Joseph's wife was Sarah Cole, daughter of Jacob.
1870, Joseph & Sarah and 5 children living in Richmond Twp, Crawford Co, PA
1880, Joseph, wife Sarah, and children living in Richmond Twp, Crawford Co, PA with
1880, Sarah is also living part of the time with son Almon and his family.

Children of Joseph Culver and Sarah Cole are:

  i. George H. Culver, born 1842 in Crawford Co, PA; died 1917.

  ii. John Eli Culver, born December 30, 1844 in Crawford Co, PA; died July 19, 1932 in 55 Penfield Ave, Akron, Summit Co, Ohio>Glendale Cemetery; married Sarah E.; born Abt. 1844.

  iii. Levi Culver, born 1848 in Crawford Co, PA.

  iv. Sarah Culver, born 1849 in Crawford Co, PA; died before 1859 in Crawford Co, Pennsylvania Mt. Hope Cemetery.

16 v. Matthias Syrus Culver, born April 01, 1853 in Washington Twp, Erie Co, PA > Crawford Co, PA; died January 01, 1898 in Blooming Valley, Crawford Co, Pennsylvania >Blooming Valley Cemetery; married Marilla "Rillie" E. Davison June 21, 1874 in Erie, Erie Co, PA.

  vi. Leon Culver, born 1855 in Crawford Co, PA.

  vii. Almon Culver, born October 24, 1857 in Crawford Co, PA; died December 24, 1906 in Hydetown, Crawford, PA>Greenwood Cemetery at Titusville, PA; married Ann M. August; born Abt. 1856.

  viii. Sarah Elizabeth Culver, born December 30, 1859 in Crawford Co, PA; died June 06, 1955 in Meadville, Crawford Co, Pennsylvania; married Mr. Davison. (see her death certificate next page).

  ix. Flora Ellen Culver, born October 15, 1865 in Crawford Co, PA; died June 30, 1929 in Townville, Crawford, Pennsylvania>Kingsley Cemetery; married George S. Smith; born December 31, 1863 in Pennsylvania; died January 31, 1947 in Meadville, Crawford Co, Pennsylvania.

  x. Alice Culver, born 1859 in Crawford Co, PA; died April 14, 1892 in Sussex Co, Delaware.

34. *Sellick Davison*, born May 24, 1836 in East Otis, Berkshire, Massachusetts; died April 22, 1922 in McLane, Erie Co, Pennsylvania. He was the son of 68. William Gordon Davison and 69. Jane Ann Maria Reed. He married 35. Mary A. Perham.

35. *Mary A. Perham*, born September 07, 1834 in New York; died November 06, 1901 in Pennsylvania. She was the daughter of 70. William Perham and 71. Mary Ann Hopkins.

Child of Sellick Davison and Mary Perham is:

17   i.   Marilla "Rillie" E. Davison, born January 21, 1857 in PA >; died May 28, 1883 in Blooming Valley, Crawford Co, PA> Blooming Valley Cemetery; married Matthias Lyrus Culver June 21, 1874 in Erie, Erie Co, PA.

36. Elijah Holt, born 1817 in New York > Edinboro, PA; died 1888 in Edinboro, Erie Co, Pennsylvania burial in Edinboro Cemetery. He married 37. Laura A. Conant.

37. Laura A. Conant, born January 28, 1820 in New York > Edinboro, PA; died 1895 in Edinboro, Erie Co, Pennsylvania burial in Edinboro Cemetery. She was the daughter of 74. Origen Conant and 75. Mary Butler.

Notes for Elijah Holt:
Find A Grave Memorial# 5765459

1840 Census, Elk Creek Twp, Erie Co, PA
1850 Census, Washington Twp, Erie Co, PA
1860 Census, Washington Twp, Erie Co, PA
1870 Census,
1880 Census, Washington Twp, Erie Co, PA

Notes for Laura A. Conant:
Find A Grave Memorial# 5765463

Children of Elijah Holt and Laura Conant are:

    18   i.   Eli Mark Holt, born April 24, 1849 in Ohio > Washington Twp, Erie Co, PA in 1900; died November 18, 1932 in Edinboro, Erie Co, Pennsylvania burial in Edinboro Cemetery; married Isabelle H. 'Belle' Wicks Bef. 1879.

                ii.   Melissa E. Holt, born March 22, 1852 in Ohio; died April 15, 1904 in Edinboro, Erie Co, Pennsylvania burial in Edinboro Cemetery.

               iii.   Mary E. Holt, born 1848 in Ohio; died 1860 in Edinboro, Erie Co, Pennsylvania burial in Edinboro Cemetery.

38. Jeremiah Smith Wicks, born January 09, 1809 in New York > McLane, Erie Co, PA; died May 21, 1889 in McLane, Erie Co, Pennsylvania > McLane Cemetery. He was the son of 76. Zophar Wicks and 77. Jane Carpenter. He married 39. Harriet Conant Bef. 1833 in New York.

39. Harriet Conant, born January 19, 1812 in New York >Washington Twp, Erie Co, PA; died June 29, 1884 in McLane, Erie Co, Pennsylvania > McLane Cemetery. She was the daughter of 74. Origen Conant and 75. Mary Butler.

Notes for Jeremiah Smith Wicks:
Find A Grave Memorial# 5365218

1860 Census: Washington Twp, Erie Co, PA

Notes for Harriet Conant:
Find A Grave Memorial# 5365219

Children of Jeremiah Wicks and Harriet Conant are:
>   i.   Loretta Wicks, born 1833 in New York.
>   ii. Samantha Wicks, born 1835 in New York.
>   iii. Clarinda Wicks, born 1837 in Erie County, PA.
>   iv. Martha Wicks, born 1839 in Erie County, PA.
>   v.   Delphia Wicks, born March 22, 1842 in Erie County, PA; died March 23, 1933 in Erie, Erie Co, PA >; married Henry Fuller; born Abt. 1841.
>   vi. Monroe Wicks, born 1846 in Erie County, PA.
> **19** vii. Isabelle H. 'Belle' Wicks, born April 18, 1847 in McLane, Erie Co, Pennsylvania; died August 06, 1934 in Edinboro, Erie Co, Pennsylvania burial in Edinboro Cemetery; married Eli Mark Holt Bef. 1879.
>   viii. Freeman Wicks, born 1854 in Erie County, PA.

40. *Mr. DeRemer* born

41. *Mrs. DeRemer* born

42. *Hazen H. Heath*, born 1812 in Massachusetts; he lived in New York State and was married there and two of their children were born in NY. Later, this family moved to Guys Mills, Crawford County, PA. Hazen died in 1891 in Crawford County and is buried at the Union Cemetery. He was the son of 84. _________ Heath and 85. _____________. He married 43. Mary E. Kane in NY state before 1834.

43. *Mary E. 'Polly' Cain* (Kane) born 1815 in New York State; she married and had two children in NY before relocating to Crawford Co, Pennsylvania. She died in 1881 at Guys Mills, Crawford Co, PA and is buried in the Union Cemetery. She was the daughter of 86. _________ Cain and 87. _________.

Burial data for Hazen H. Heath:
Find A Grave Memorial# 17844446

Burial data for Mary Polly Kane:
Find A Grave Memorial# 17844452

Children of Hazen Heath & Polly Cain:
>   i   William H. Heath Born: 1834 in New York
>   ii   Elmira E. Heath Born: 1836 in New York
>   iii Mary Heath   Born: 1838 in New York
>   iv   Phebe Heath   Born: 1842 in Crawford Co, PA

21 v Irena Heath Born: August 03, 1843 in Crawford Co, PA Died: May 4, 1921. She married Levi DeRemer Born: December 24, 1840 in New York
    vi Sarah E. Heath Born: 1845 in Crawford Co, PA
    vii Nathan C. Heath Born: 1848 in Crawford Co, PA
    viii Ira Heath Born: 1850 in Crawford Co, PA
    ix Byron Heath Born: 1854 in Crawford Co, PA

44. *John Ambrose Clark* born in 1819 in Pennsylvania; he died __________ at ____________. He was the son of 88. _________ Clark and _________. He married 45. Dorcas Hoffman.

45. *Dorcas Hoffman*, born in 1815 in Pennsylvania; died ________ at _____________. She was the daughter of 90. ______ Hoffman and 91.___________.

More on John & Dorcas Clark:
1850 Census, John A. Clark age 30 and wife, Dorcas age 34 are living in Union Twp, Erie Co, PA. No children yet.
1860 Census, John & family were living in Meadville, Wayne Twp, Crawford Co, PA. 5 children.
1870 Census, John and 3 sons, Andrew, Jacob, Robert, are living in Steuben Twp, Crawford Co, PA - Dorcas not listed - did she die?

Child of Jacob Clark is:
  22 i. Jacob Clark, born March 1854 in Crawford Co, PA; married Jenny Mae Coy in 1877 in Pennsylvania.
    ii. Margaret E. Clark born August 17, 1851 in Union City, PA, she married Mr. Brightman; Margaret died Jan. 11, 1923 in Titusville, PA.
    iii. Andrew Clark born 1852 in PA
    iv. Robert Clark born 1857 in PA
    v. Delight Clark born 1859 in PA
    vi. John C. Clark born 1862 in PA, married Alice A. Sterns Wallace.

46. *George Coy*, born March 4, 1821 in PA and lived at Guys Mills, Crawford Co, Pennsylvania; he died January 20, 1899 at Blooming Valley Crawford Co, PA and buried in the Blooming Valley Cemetery. He was the son of 92. _________Coy and 93.___________. He married 47. Mary Jane Knapp.

47. *Mary Jane Knapp*, born January 13, 1825 in Woodcock Twp, Crawford Co, Pennsylvania; and died on April 4, 1874 at Woodcock Twp, Crawford County. She is buried in the Blooming Valley Cemetery. She was the daughter of 94. Arba Knapp and 95. Civillia Britton.

Burial info for George Coy:
Find A Grave Memorial# 39086168
Burial info for Mary Jane Knapp:
Find A Grave Memorial# 153274542

Children of George Coy and Amelia Mary are:

	i.	Cevilla Coy, born 1847 in Pennsylvania; died 1873.
	ii.	Olive Coy, born 1849 in Pennsylvania.
	iii.	Frank Coy, born 1852 in Pennsylvania.
23	iv.	Jenny Mae Coy, born 1857 in Pennsylvania; died 1920; married Jacob C. Clark Bef. 1877 in Pennsylvania.
	v.	James Coy, born 1875 in Pennsylvania.

56. *Joel Tyson Umstead*, born 1783; died Abt. 1870. Joel was the son of 112. _________ Umstead and 113. ____________. He married 57. Anna Tyson Hunsberger.

57. *Anna Tyson Hunsberger*, born Abt. 1784; died in Neiffer, Montgomery Co, PA >Herstine Mennonite Church Cemetery. She was the daughter of 114. Abraham Hunsberger and 115. Catherine Nash Tyson.

Child of Joel Umstead and Anna Hunsberger is:

28	i.	Jacob Hunsberger Umstead, born October 18, 1809 in Illinois City, PA; died January 24, 1894 in Oil City, Venango Co, PA >Grove Hill Cemetery; married (1) Elizabeth Reed Abt. 1830; married (2) Barbara Johnston Herstine Abt. 1846 in Pennsylvania.

62.   *William Harrison Manross*, born October 24, 1816 in Bradford Co, Pennsylvania; died July 19, 1893 in Venango Co, PA and is buried at Brandon Cemetery in Brandon, PA. William was the son of 124. _________ Manross and 125. ______________. A Civil War Veteran. He married 63. Margaret Callen Brandon.

63. *Margaret Callen Brandon*, born 1818 in Clarion Co, Pennsylvania; died August 27, 1895 in Venango Co, PA and is buried in Brandon Cemetery at Brandon, Venango Co, PA. She was the daughter of 126. Elliott Brandon from Ireland, and 127. Miss Callen.

Burial Data for William Manross:
Find A Grave Memorial# 103092739
Burial Data for Margaret Brandon:
Find A Grave Memorial# 103092681

Children of William Manross and Margaret Callen are:

    i.   John Manross, born Abt. 1838 in Venango Co, PA; died 1865 in Brandon, Venango, PA Brandon Cemetery.

    ii.   Elliott Manross, born January 16, 1840 in Venango Co, PA; died 1924 in Brandon, Venango, PA Brandon Cemetery; married Sarah Jane Morrison; born 1846; died 1922.

    iii.   Ira Manross, born August 08, 1841 in Venango Co, PA; died September 22, 1914 in Reno, Venango PA >Brandon Cemetery.

    iv.   Samantha Belle Manross, born 1844 in Venango Co, PA.

    v.   Sarah E. 'Sally' Manross, born October 07, 1846 in Venango Co, PA; died April 14, 1916; married Jacob Miles Foreman; born Abt. 1845.

    vi.   Angeline Manross, born 1850 in Venango Co, PA.

    vii.   William C. Manross, born Abt. 1852 in Venango Co, PA.

31   viii.   Female Manross, born Bet. 1840 - 1850 in Venango Co, PA; married John Bell.

Generation No. 7

(Great Great Great Great Grandparents)
Found: 18 of 64

64. Joseph Sr. Culver, born July 19, 1794 in Weatherfield Twp, Windsor Co, Vermont; died February 23, 1847 in Spartansburg, Crawford Co, Pennsylvania. He was the son of 128. Jonathan Culver and 129. Annah Gilson. He married 65. Pheba Johnston August 12, 1819 in Norfolk, St. Lawrence, New York. Joseph married a 2nd time to Mary Wood in Ohio on June 21, 1842.

65. Pheba Johnston, born February 05, 1803 in Ellsburg, Jefferson Co, New York; She was the daughter of 130. ________ Johnston and 131. ________. Pheba died February 17, 1839 in Johnston, Trumbull, Ohio.

Notes for Joseph Sr. Culver:
1820 Census: living in Louisville, Saint Lawrence Co, New York, wife and 2 children
1840 Census: living in Johnston, Trumbull County, Ohio; eleven in household; 7 male children, Joseph age 40-50; 1 male age 70-80; 1 female age 15-20; 1 female age 60-70. [probably his parents, Jonathan & Annah Culver were living with Joseph]

Children of Joseph Culver and Pheba Johnston are:

    i.   Nathan B. Culver, born 1820 in Louisville, Saint Lawrence Co, NY; died 1896.

32   ii.   Joseph H. Culver, born October 20, 1822 in Wilkes Farm, Crawford Co, PA; died September 16, 1893 in Townville, Crawford Co, PA >Kingsley Cemetery; married Sarah Cole Bef. 1842 in Crawford Co, PA.

iii. Ann B. Culver, born 1824; died 1909.
iv. Warren Culver, born 1826.
v. Elvarious B. Culver, born February 06, 1827 in Norfolk, New York; died 1912; married Ruby Oliver; born Abt. 1830.
vi. Catherine W. Culver, born November 06, 1829 in Cambridge, Washington, NY; died April 12, 1915 in Cook Co, Illinois >burial in Iowa City, Iowa; married James Truesdell May 19, 1868 in Iowa City, Johnson Co, Iowa; born February 05, 1814 in Newton, Sussex, NJ; died February 08, 1885 in What Cheer, Keokuk, Iowa.
vii. Cornelius Culver, born 1831.
viii. Darius Alden Culver, born 1833; died 1912.
ix. Charles Albert Culver, born 1835; died 1897.
x. Jonah Byron Culver, born 1838; died 1905.

66. *Jacobus 'Jacob' Cole*, born 1784 in New York > Crawford Co, PA; died June 06, 1864 in Woodcock Twp, Crawford Co, PA > Mount Blair Cemetery. He was the son of 132. George Kohl Cole and 133. Margaret Krug. He married 67. **Rachel** Bef. 1822.

67. *Rachel* ___________, born 1787 in New York > Crawford Co, PA; died March 26, 1854 in Woodcock Twp, Crawford Co, PA >Mount Blair Cemetery.

Notes for Jacobus 'Jacob' Cole:
Find A Grave Memorial# 48937241

1850 Census: living in Richmond Twp, Crawford Co, PA. Jacob, Rachel and Matthias all born in NY. Henry born in PA.
1860 Census: living alone in Richmond Twp, Crawford Co, Pennsylvania, age 73, wife, Rachel, died in 1854. Next door his son, Michael Cole age 33 lives with his family; two houses down lives another son with his family, Mathias Cole age 35. On the other side of his residence, is his daughter & her husband, Joseph Culver and family.

Notes for Rachel ________:
Find A Grave Memorial# 48937256

Children of Jacobus Cole and Rachel are:
33   i. Sarah Cole, born 1822 in New York > Crawford Co, PA; died September 1880 in Townville, Crawford Co, PA >Kingsley Cemetery; married Joseph H. Culver Bef. 1842 in Crawford Co, PA.
ii. Michael Cole, born 1828 in Blooming Valley, Crawford Co, PA; died February 03, 1892 in Pleasantville, Venango Co, PA >Fairview Cemetery; married Sarah Jane Ryan; born April 07, 1830 in Blooming Valley, Crawford Co, PA; died May 08, 1917 in Pleasantville, Venango Co, PA >Fairview Cemetery.

Notes for Michael Cole:
Find A Grave Memorial# 9427172
Notes for Sarah Jane Ryan:
Find A Grave Memorial# 155096179

   iii.   Mathias Cole, born 1825 in New York > Crawford Co, PA; died 1915 in Pleasantville, Venango Co, PA >Fairview Cemetery; married Elizabeth Jane Widger Bef. 1851 in Crawford Co, PA; born January 13, 1829 in Manch Chuck, Crawford Co, PA; died January 25, 1918 in Pleasantville, Venango Co, PA >Fairview Cemetery.
Notes for Mathias Cole:
Find A Grave Memorial# 8861009

   iv.   Henry Cole, born 1834 in Crawford Co, PA.

68.   William Gordon Davison, born March 15, 1804 in East Otis, Berkshire, Massachusetts; died March 02, 1880 in Richmont Twp, Crawford Co, PA. He was the son of 136. John Davison and 137. Lydia Wood. He married 69. Jane Ann Maria Reed.

69.   Jane Ann Maria Reed, born July 15, 1811 in New York; died October 12, 1880 in Pennsylvania. She was the daughter of 138. Eliphalet Reed and 139. Anne Sackett.

Child of William Davison and Jane Reed is:

  34   i.   Sellick Davison, born May 24, 1836 in East Otis, Berkshire, Massachusetts; died April 22, 1922 in McLane, Erie Co, Pennsylvania; married Mary A. Perham.

70.   William Perham, born January 21, 1808 in Vermont; died June 21, 1879 in Chikaming, Berrien, Michigan. He married 71. Mary Ann Hopkins.

71.   Mary Ann Hopkins, born 1812 in New York; died 1891 in Three Oaks, Berrien, Michigan.

Child of William Perham and Mary Hopkins is:

  35   i.   Mary A. Perham, born September 07, 1834 in New York; died November 06, 1901 in Pennsylvania; married Sellick Davison.

74.   Origen Conant, born 1786 in Alleghany County, New York; died 1839 in Waterbury, Washington Co, Vermont. He was the son of 148. Benjamin Conant and 149. Ruth. He married 75. Mary Butler.

75. *Mary Butler,* born September 11, 1790 in New York; died May 12, 1870 in Warwick, Franklin Co, Massachusetts.

Children of Origen Conant and Mary Butler are: (Notice that you have two sets of grandparents for these siblings)

39   i.   Harriet Conant, born January 19, 1812 in New York >Washington Twp, Erie Co, PA; died June 29, 1884 in McLane, Erie Co, Pennsylvania > McLane Cemetery; married **Jeremiah Smith Wicks** Bef. 1833 in New York.

37   ii.   Laura A. Conant, born January 28, 1820 in New York > Edinboro, PA; died 1895 in Edinboro, Erie Co, Pennsylvania burial in Edinboro Cemetery; married **Elijah Holt**.

76. *Zophar Wicks,* born October 09, 1755 in Huntington, Suffolk, New York; died August 20, 1847 in Roxbury, Delaware, New York. He married 77. Jane Carpenter.

77. *Jane Carpenter,* born March 19, 1763 in New York; died September 30, 1856 in New York.

Child of Zophar Wicks and Jane Carpenter is:

38   i.   Jeremiah Smith Wicks, born January 09, 1809 in New York > McLane, Erie Co, PA; died May 21, 1889 in McLane, Erie Co, Pennsylvania > McLane Cemetery; married Harriet Conant Bef. 1833 in New York.

88. *Jacob Clark Sr,*

89. *Mrs. Clark __________,*

Child of Jacob Clark is:

44   i.   Jacob Clark, Jr.

114. *Abraham Hunsberger,* born October 04, 1755 in Perkiomen, Philadelphia Co, Pennsylvania; died February 23, 1816 in Limerick, Montgomery Co, PA. He married 115. Catherine Nash Tyson 1779.

115. *Catherine Nash Tyson,* born January 03, 1760; died June 21, 1819.

Child of Abraham Hunsberger and Catherine Tyson is:

57   i.   Anna Tyson Hunsberger, born Abt. 1784; died in Neiffer, Montgomery Co, PA >Herstine Mennonite Church Cemetery; married Joel Tyson Umstead.

126. _Elliott Brandon_, born in c.1785 in Ireland; he died after 1860 in Sugarcreek Twp, Venango Co, Pennsylvania. Elliott was the son of 252. James Brandon and 253. Mary Elliott. He married 127. Sarah Callen.

127. _Sarah Callen_, born c.1785 in Pennsylvania, she died on ______ at ______________, burial at __________. Sarah was the daughter of 254. Patrick Callen and 255. Sarah Hennen Hearney.

VENANGO COUNTY DEED BOOK G; 224
Know all men by these presents that we Elliott Brandon and Sarah his wife for and in consideration of the sum of three hundred dollars to them in hand have granted bargained and sold at their as our right title interest and claim of in and to the within Deed to James Brandon and we hereby for ourselves heirs and assigns concedes and convey to the said James Brandon our whole wright and title to him his heirs and assigns as fully to all intents and purposes as the same is vested by the within deed to him and his heirs forever. In testimony whereof we have here unto let our lands and Seals the eleventh day of July 1826. Witness at Signing; John Bradfoot, Elliott Brandon, Sarah Brandon

Child of Elliott Brandon and Callen is:

   63   i.   Margaret Callen Brandon, born 1818 in Clarion Co, Pennsylvania; died August 27, 1895 in Venango Co, PA; married William Harrison Manross.

Generation No. 8

(Fifth Great Grandparents)
Found: 14 of 128

128. _Jonathan Culver_, born 1766 in Vermont and relocated to Norfolk, St. Lawrence, New York where he was a prominent member of the area, building dams and mills, etc. Jonathan journeyed westward with his son, Joseph, and died sometime between 1840-1850 in Trumbull County Ohio. Jonathan was the son of 256. __________ Culver and 257. _____________. He married 129. Annah Breed Gilson.

129. _Annah Breed Gilson_, born February 2, 1762-68 in Westminster, Windham County, Vermont. She died June 13, 1854 in Platteville, Grant Co, Wisconsin and is buried in the Whig Cemetery there. She was the daughter of 258. Zachariah Gilson of

Vermont. Annah went to Wisconsin with her daughter, Annah and her family, after Jonathan Culver died.

Notes on Jonathan Culver born in 1766 in VT:
On November 15, 1825, Norfolk, St. Lawrence Co, New York, Jonathan Culver filed a patent for an invention called "Shingles, a machine for sawing (shingles)"
"The first dam and mills were built here [Norfolk, NY] by Jonathan Culver in 1815. The dam was swept away in December, 1847 and another was built near the same place in 1848." [1]
"The first grist mill was built by Jonathan Culver, on Racket River, three miles below Raymondville, in 1812. It contained a single run of stones, and was afterwards burned."

Child of Jonathan Culver is:

64   i.   Joseph Sr. Culver, born July 19, 1794 in Weatherfield Twp, Windsor Co, Vermont; died February 23, 1847 in Spartansburg, Crawford Co, PA; married (1) Pheba Johnston August 12, 1819 in Norfolk, St. Lawrence, New York; married (2) Mary Wood 1842 in Ohio.

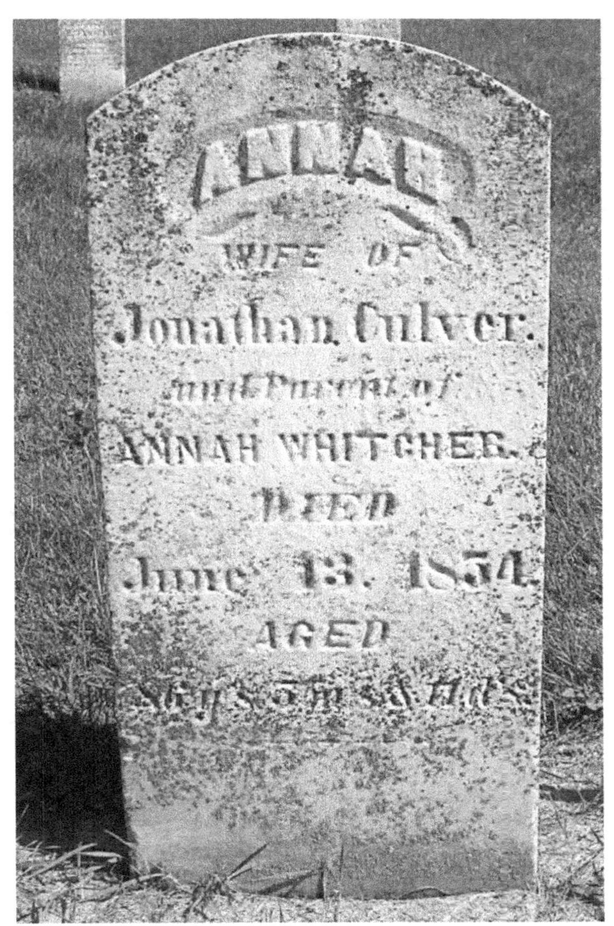

BIRTH—FEMALE

Name of Child	Annah Gilson	
Color		No. of Child of Mother
Date of Birth	February Month 2 Day 17	
Maiden Name of Mother		
Mother's Birthplace		Age
Mother's Residence		
Full Name of Father	Zachariah Gilson	
Father's Birthplace		Age
Father's Occupation		
Condition of Child as to Live or Still Birth	Live Still	
If Still Birth the Cause		
Name of Informant		
Town Westminster	John Sessions Town Clerk	

132.   George Kohl Cole, born 1751 in Darmstadt, Hessen, Germany; died December 31, 1842 in Adams Co, Pennsylvania. He married 133. Margaret Krug.

133. Margaret Krug, born Abt. 1752.

Child of George Cole and Margaret Krug is:

    66   i.   Jacobus 'Jacob' Cole, born 1784 in New York > Crawford Co, PA; died June 06, 1864 in Woodcock Twp, Crawford Co, PA > Mount Blair Cemetery; married Rachel Bef. 1822.

136. John Davison, born 1763; died 1842. He married 137. Lydia Wood.

137. Lydia Wood, born 1770; died 1853.

Child of John Davison and Lydia Wood is:

    68   i.   William Gordon Davison, born March 15, 1804 in East Otis, Berkshire, Massachusetts; died March 02, 1880 in Richmond Twp, Crawford Co, PA; married Jane Ann Maria Reed.

138. Eliphalet Reed, born June 11, 1758 in Windham Co, Connecticut. He was the son of 276. David Reed and 277. Waitstill Raynsford. He married 139. Anne Sackett.

139. Anne Sackett, born 1781 in Newton, Long Island, NY; died September 20, 1757 in Newton, Long Island, NY. She was the daughter of 278. Joseph Sackett and 279. Elizabeth Betts.

Child of Eliphalet Reed and Anne Sackett is:

    69   i.   Jane Ann Maria Reed, born July 15, 1811 in New York; died October 12, 1880 in Pennsylvania; married William Gordon Davison.

140.-147. Not Found

148. Benjamin Conant, born 1760 in Scotland; immigrated to America and first came to Westmoreland, New Hampshire, then relocating to Alleghany Co, New York. He married 149. Ruth ___________. [2]

149. Ruth ___________, born c.1761 in Ireland.

Children of Benjamin Conant and Ruth are:

    74   i.   Origen Conant, born 1786 in Alleghany County, New York; died 1839 in Waterbury, Washington Co, Vermont; married Mary Butler.
           ii.   Josiah Conant
          iii. Shubael Conant
          iv. Olive Conant
           v. Electa Conant
          vi. Clarissa Conant
         vii. Sally Conant

252. James Brandon,

253. Mary Elliott,

They were the parents of:

    126   i.   Elliott Brandon, born ___________; - he married Sarah Cullen.

254. Patrick Cullen,

255. Sarah Hearney,

---

[2] A History and Genealogy of the Conant Family in England and America, Thirteen Generations, 1520-1887: Containing Also Some Genealogical Notes on the Connet, Connett and Connit Families

They were the parents of:

127   i.   Sarah Cullen, born _________; she married Elliott Brandon

Generation No. 9

(Sixth Great Grandparents)
Found: 8 of 256

256. _______ **Culver**, born c.1735

257. _______**Mrs. Culver**, born c.1741

They were the parents of:
128   i.   Jonathan Culver born 1766 in Vermont; died 1840-1850 in Ohio, married Annah Gilson.

258. Zachariah Gilson, born January 14, 1736 in Vermont; died November 15, 1804 at Westminster, Windham Co, Vermont, burial in the Gilson Cemetery. He married Annah Patch.

259. Annah Patch, born in 1743 in Vermont; she died on November 8, 1826 at Westminster, Windham Co, Vermont and buried in the Gilson Cemetery.

They were the parents of:
129   i.   Annah Gilson born Feb 2, 1762-68 in Westminster, VT; she married Jonathan Culver.

276. David Reed, born 1725 in Windsor, Hartford, CT; died 1828 in Sheffield, Berkshire, Massachusetts. He married 277. Waitstill Raynsford.

277. Waitstill Raynsford, born February 18, 1741 in Canterbury, Windham, CT; died October 13, 1785 in Massachusetts.

Child of David Reed and Waitstill Raynsford is:
138   i.   Eliphalet Reed, born June 11, 1758 in Winham Co, Connecticut; married
            Anne Sackett.

278. Joseph Sackett, born February 23, 1656 in Springfield, Hampden, MA; died September 23, 1719 in Long Island City, Queens, NY. He married 279. Elizabeth Betts.

279.   Elizabeth Betts, born 1658 in Newton, Long Island, NY; died 1701 in Newton, Long Island, NY.

Child of Joseph Sackett and Elizabeth Betts is:

    139   i.   Anne Sackett, born 1681 in Newton, Long Island, NY; died September 20, 1757 in Newton, Long Island, NY; married Eliphalet Reed.

Addition Culver Family Genealogy: https://archive.org/details/colverculvergene00colv